LANGUA

Rod Mengham lectures at the
where he is a Fellow of and Dir
at Jesus College.

LANGUAGE

ROD MENGHAM

Fontana Press
An imprint of HarperCollins*Publishers*

Fontana Press
An Imprint of HarperCollins*Publishers*
77–85 Fulham Palace Road,
Hammersmith, London W6 8JB

Published by Fontana Press 1995
1 3 5 7 9 8 6 4 2

First published in Great Britain by
Bloomsbury 1993

The author and publisher would like to thank the following
for allowing the reproduction of copyright images:

University College Dublin Library (p.10); Mary Evans Picture Library
(p. 20, p. 145); Bridgeman Art Library (p. 38); Museo Archeologico
Nazionale, Napoli (p. 82); United Distillers UK plc (p.163)

ISBN 0 00 654499 1

Set in Bembo

Printed in Great Britain by
HarperCollinsManufacturing Glasgow

CONTENTS

Introduction: Hearing voices, seeing signs 1

1 Syntax and circuitry: language, mind and brain 15

2 Graphic equalizer: language in writing and speech 27

3 The curse from Babel: the distribution of languages 51

4 On parole: language in society 75

5 Worlds of words: universal grammars, encyclopaedic dictionaries 99

6 Ties of the tongue: language, nation, class and gender 121

7 The debt to meaning: language and money 141

8 The curse of babble: the language of distribution 159

Notes 179

Bibliography 182

Index 185

LIST OF ILLUSTRATIONS

page 1	Cave painting 13,000 BC, Fount de Gaume, south-west France
page 10	The novelist James Joyce
page 15	Ugaritic abecedary
page 20	Phrenological head
page 27	Egyptian hieroglyphics
page 38	The Rosetta Stone
page 51	Cretan Linear B script
page 71	Fragment of the Habakkuk commentary, Dead Sea Scrolls
page 75	Phoenician script
page 82	Pompeian fresco
page 99	Ancient Greek inscription (cup of Nestor)
page 104	Title page, *An Introduction to the Universal Language* by Sir Thomas Urquhart
page 121	Chinese script
page 129	Thackeray's sketch of Dr Johnson and Oliver Goldsmith
page 141	Japanese script
page 145	Ancient Greek coins and Gutenberg typeface
page 159	Cherokee script
page 163	Advertisement for White Horse whisky (1970s)

INTRODUCTION

HEARING VOICES, SEEING SIGNS

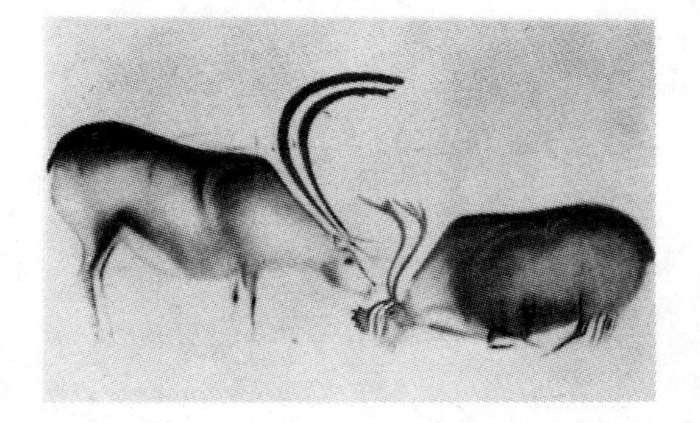

INTRODUCTION

HEARING VOICES, SEEING SIGNS

> Therfor was callid the name of it Babel, for there was confoundid the lippe of all the erthe.
>
> Genesis 11:9, translated by John Wyclif (1382)

The Tower of Babel. The idea of this building, which has gripped the imagination of artists and writers for thousands of years, represents both the pinnacle of linguistic ambition and the height from which real languages are judged to have fallen. The crazy attempt to erect a structure that might bridge the gap between earth and heaven shows the depth and intensity of a human need, the need to be furnished with a language that not only matches the world of physical phenomena, but which in some sense brings that world into existence. In the language of God, words have creative power, and the biblical formula 'In the beginning was the Word' suggests the extent to which consciousness of the world only springs into being with the utterance, or inscription, of those words that give us names for it.

The descent from the Tower, then, is like another Fall: a decline into anarchy and linguistic isolation. And yet the instant of chaos in the biblical myth stands for nothing less than the whole of human history, for the process of gradual divergence, and occasional re-convergence, of multifarious linguistic traditions. The ascent and descent of the builders of Babel reflects the preoccupations of this book, in which the human muddle rather than the originary ideal of language is viewed as its creative source, as the true condition in which to construct a sense of identity and relationship. The movement back down to earth, in other words, is taken as the positive trajectory; and in turning over the many facets of language development in the histories of societies and the lives of individuals I have concentrated on another side of meaning reflected in the word 'descent': 'derivation from an ancestral stock; lineage; transmission by inheritance'.

If I have returned to an early-established model of linguistic evolution, that of the family tree, this is because much of the historical material I discuss is itself predicated on a belief in the kinds of continuities and variations that are shaped in the momentum of family histories. Family history is a social concept that can be repressively insisted on or subversively challenged with the possibilities of innovative change. It is never entirely remote from this discussion, which places language within a variety of social frameworks and historical phases in order to explore the kind of linguistic space mapped out in remarks made by the American linguist Edward Sapir:

> It is quite an illusion to imagine that one adjusts to reality, essentially without the use of language and that language is merely an individual means of solving specific problems of communication or reflection. The fact of the matter is that the 'real world' is to a large extent unconsciously built up on the language habits of the group . . . . We see and hear and otherwise experience very largely as we do because the language habits of our community predispose certain choices of interpretation.[1]

Sapir's view of the role of language in human societies is as authoritative as it is widely shared. But at a time when scientific research has shown that certain elements of language pre-exist social organization and when humankind itself has devised and generated artificial languages that have extended their reach over many of the most important areas of our lives, Sapir's proposition offers a starting point, and not the last word, in an urgent and vital debate about the place of language in the world.

William Golding's novel *The Inheritors*, which tries to

imagine the life of prehistoric societies, provides as effective an impression as any of what it might have been like to experience the world without language, or rather with only the beginnings of language. This is Golding's description of a Neanderthal group gathered round a fire:

> As they persuaded themselves of the warmth they relaxed limbs and drew reek into their nostrils gratefully. They flexed their toes and stretched their arms, even leaning away from the fire. One of the deep silences fell on them, that seemed so much more natural than speech, a timeless silence in which there were at first many minds in the overhang; and then perhaps no mind at all. So fully discounted was the roar of the water that the soft touch of the wind on the rocks became audible. Their ears as if endowed with separate life sorted the tangle of tiny sounds and accepted them, the sound of breathing, the sound of wet clay flaking and ashes falling in.[2]

Despite the eloquence of Golding's own prose, what is successfully evoked here is a world that is almost empty of thought, all but deprived of analysis. The Neanderthals inhabit a universe in which they are open to visual, tactile, and aural stimuli, but which they cannot organize conceptually. Without a language with tenses that determine the differences between past, present and future, and without the means of defining the limits of personal agency, they cannot relate phenomena through time and in space. In habitual silence, many minds coalesce into one mind, which is like no mind. As far as one can tell, the life of a Neanderthal would be radically discontinuous, a process of being bombarded by fragments of experience not even searching for, let alone finding, a meaningful context.

We know of course, that everything changed, but how did it change, and why did both people and language follow the particular path of development that they did? Golding's narration is placed, imaginatively, in the position of *homo erectus*. What was the selection pressure in the anthropoid brain that produced the new strain of *homo sapiens*? It may be that the evolution of mind and brain should be seen primarily as a process of interaction with language, that the creation of language was the creation of the selection pressure which actually allowed the cerebral cortex and consciousness of self to develop.

At the other end of the story, which is where we may be, a mutation of consciousness is expected in the linguistic breakdowns of a post-technological retreat from historical forms of society. Russell Hoban's novel *Riddley Walker* imagines a post-holocaust landscape sparsely inhabited by survivors whose intellectual deprivation is linked directly to the poverty of their language:

> Lorna said to me 'You know Riddley theres some thing in us it dont have no name.'
>
> I said, 'What thing is that?'
>
> She said, 'Its some kynd of thing it aint us but yet its in us. Its looking out thru our eye hoals. May be you dont take no noatis of it only some times. Say you get woak up suddn in the middl of the nite. I minim youre a sleap and the nex youre on your feet with a spear in your han. Wel it wernt you put that spear in your han it wer the other thing whats looking out thru your eye hoals. It aint you nor it dont even know your name. Its in us lorn and loan and sheltering how it can.'
>
> I said, 'If its in every one of us of us theres moren one of it theres got to be a manying theres got to be a millying and mor.'
>
> Lorna said, 'Wel there is a millying and mor.'
>
> I said, 'Wel if theres such a manying of it whys it lorn then whys it loan?'
>
> She said, 'Becaws the manying and the millying its all one thing it dont have nothing to gether with. You look at lykens on a stoan its all them tiny manyings of it and may be each part of it myt think its sepert only we can see its all one thing . . .'[3]

This inability to give a name to the life-force or spirit which the characters have obscure inklings of, is the reverse of the Adamic situation in which language consists of a set of terms designating things in the world in a completely unproblematic fashion. In Hoban's projection concepts begin to drift away from the mind as the names for them drop out of language. The struggle to determine the limits of personal agency, the doubts about whether one names or is named by the 'some thing' beyond one, reflects the inchoate thinking of the Neanderthals in Golding's novel. In both cases, the elementary quality of the perception or articulation makes for good fiction, because of the characters' reliance on the concrete, on the physical co-ordinates that determine their apprehension of the world. Hoban's characters are immature, but the language of his text is not; it is rather a debasement of standard contemporary English that represents a kind of second Fall, or 'descent' of language in which words became unreliable carriers of meaning. The reader is clearly intended to compare Riddley's regressive form of speech with a more familiar syntax in which the relationship between language and reality seems less uncertain, less provisional. The contrast between the solitary individual and the multitude, between the 'lorn and loan' and the 'millying and the mor' emphasizes the omission of an intermediate realm in which most social relationships find their appropriate scale. It is in this intermediate realm that language normally operates as the fundamental medium of expression, communication, commemoration.

As I have said, this book will be chiefly concerned with the sense in which social reality has been governed by a genealogical 'descent' of language. It will consider the area between the pre-historic and the post-historic, the interval within which languages have been developed in a form of lineage, in families and groups, providing societies with a framework for stability as well as successive opportunities for variation and change. Although the argument will cover issues of differentiation and distribution common to many languages, the majority of illustrations will be taken from English, and especially English literature. One particular reason to focus on English is its already very widespread and growing use as a medium of international communications, which makes it important to appreciate the extent to which the history of the language is the history of its involvement with politics, religion, class, gender, nation, race and more.

Studying the history of language may involve an exclusive concentration on the development of linguistic structures, but it may just as well lead to an awareness of certain aspects of history in general that can only ever be recovered *through* language. Of course, the retrieval of past social forms and models of consciousness from the evidence of language and language alone is a fallible process, above all because it is possible to project the concerns of the present back into the textual material of the past. However, I should like to try and show, by examining part of one particular text, that structure and history are always interrelated, and that although contextual knowledge is always welcome, there is always a facet or facets of a given text that will reflect an appropriate context however well hidden. What needs to be gauged is the extent to which the text will always imply its context.

The celebrated ending of James Joyce's short story 'The Dead' supplies an occasion for comparing the implications of its language with the explicit information of contextual knowledge specialized enough not to be commonly found (and not found at all in my experience) in criticism of the text:

> The time had come for him to set out on his journey westward. Yes, the newspapers were right: snow was general all over Ireland. It was falling on every part of the dark central plain, on the treeless hills, falling softly on the Bog of Allen and, farther westward, softly falling into the dark mutinous Shannon waves. It was falling, too, on every part of the lonely churchyard on the hill where Michael Furey lay buried. It lay thickly drifted on the crooked crosses and headstones, on the spears of the little gate, on the barren thorns. His soul swooned slowly as he heard the snow falling faintly through the universe and faintly falling, like the descent of their last end, upon all the living and the dead.[4]

This is the final passage in the story whose explorations of the differences between Englishness and Irishness, and between the past and the present, touch on all the issues I have already mentioned, of politics, religion, class, gender, nation and race.

The focal point of the passage is a shift from individual self-consciousness to the projection of a general condition. The individual in question, Gabriel Conroy, is the most Anglicized character in the story, while his wife, Gretta, stands for a certain idea of Irishness. Husband and wife have spent the evening at a Christmas party where Gabriel has delivered a hypocritical speech on the conditions of Irish hospitality. They are both now in a hotel room where Gabriel learns of Gretta's girlhood passion for the romantic peasant figure of the dead Michael Furey. Occasional contrasts between other characters representing Protestantism and Catholicism, English authoritarianism and Irish nationalism, give a political undertone to the story.

The brilliance of Joyce's writing is to make this political dimension insistent and all-pervasive, never hysterical or over-emphasized. Gabriel's mind is constantly slipping away from the settling of the party in order to contemplate the image of snow setting on the Wellington monument, an English power symbol which Gabriel, in imagination, is constantly drawn towards and hovers around. His mental paralysis is one symptom of the morbid condition that is contemporary Irishness. The story as a whole is congested, as its title suggests it would be, with allusions both to those who are already dead, and to those who are, in their various ways, close to morbidity.

The overview of the last paragraph is controlled by an evocation of the snow which gradually smothers and extinguishes all life, settling on the tombstones which respond with their own symbolism of death, and suggesting a condition which is inescapable since the snow is 'general all over Ireland' and alike upon 'all the living and the dead', as if there is no important distinction to made between these.

The final extension of Gabriel's awareness, blurring the distinction between the living and the dead, represents a double yielding on his part, since not only is the west symbolic of expiration (it is where the sun sets), it is also the heartland of an anachronistic nationalism. Gabriel's contemplation of an entropic universe from the vantage point of his hotel window includes the division into inside

James Joyce in the Curran family garden, 1904.

and outside, warmth and cold, that has been present throughout the text. The absorption of his imagination into a world of frozen nullity has been prefigured by his flights of fancy, preferring the idea of the cold outside and of the solitary Wellington monument to the warmth and fellowship of the party inside the house. The notion of warmth is employed adverbially throughout the story to indicate moments of excitable dissension from dominant or standard points of view. Whether it is experienced as sexual passion or as a readiness for argument, warmth is seen as potentially subversive, a possible means of melting, of dissolving, the qualities that come to be associated with the falling of the snow, qualities of frigidity, inflexibility, lifelessness. The condition of Ireland is determined by the settling, the sedimenting, of attitudes into a form with which it becomes impossible to negotiate. Irish lives are seen as being lived in terms of a narrative of their involvement with the Roman Catholic church, British Imperialism, and Irish nationalism. Joyce's concern is to defy the claims and patterns of that narrative order by loosening its hold upon the material, by introducing a political dimension to his text at every available point.

In the final paragraph, the political dimension is unmistakeable. The special contextual knowledge that is not revealed in the writing but which, once it is restored to view, confirms the tendentiousness of Joyce's poetic prose, concerns the most traumatic event in Irish history. The description of the snow encroaching on the whole of Ireland resembles accounts of the coming of the Great Famine in 1846. Compare this version by the Reverend John O'Rourke, who records that the potato blight was ushered in by 'a most singular cloud . . . an extremely white vapour, resembling a snow-storm . . . . It was noticed in various districts that some two days before the disease appeared on the potatoes, a dense cloud resembling a thick fog overspread the entire country . . . .'[5] The Famine divided the history of the country into two, and marked the suffering of the Irish with an indelible sense of ill-use by the British. The loss of life was heaviest in Galway, an area in the west of the country where we are told Gretta had hoped to take her holiday. Above all, the Famine was regarded as a 'terrible legacy' to subsequent generations, an inheritance of political resentment that would forever affect the 'descent' of the Irish and their use of the English language.

The spectre of the Famine haunts the passage without actually materializing, but the issues it raises are all touched on in the contrast between east and west, mutiny and anaesthesia as well as in symbolic references to Catholic martyrdom ('spears' and 'thorns'), and in the stress on links between past, present, and future generations, the importance of parallels being suggested by the repetitiveness of some of the language. Joyce's text provides a demonstration of how far the history of a society speaks through the language chosen by an individual writer to express apparently personal concerns. The great American linguist Benjamin Lee Whorf argued that the personal mind, which can select words but is largely unaware of pattern, should be thought of as being held in the grip of a higher, far more intellectual mind which 'can systematize and mathematize on a scale and scope that no mathematician of the schools ever remotely approached'. This is almost to conceive of language as a separate intelligence that works through, or expresses itself by means of, the linguistic competence of individual humans. For the most part, I am interested in the social parameters of this kind of interception of human activity, although I recognize that Whorf's conception of language allows for other modes of operation. It is in dealing with language that humankind tests the nature of its relation with spirit, experiences language as the hearing of voices, the seeing of signs indicative of a quality that cannot easily be reduced to sense or rendered translatable. This possibility, which echoes the 'silence more natural than speech' of Golding and 'the something in us, it dont have no name' of Hoban, has been constantly on the horizon of language development.

On the other hand, the possibility that language somehow exists outside the interpersonal sphere, modelling individual human subjects according to a kind of blueprint that pre-exists them, is amenable to a biological emphasis. It is, after all, certain that the symbiosis of language and mind is profound enough to have played a crucial role in the physiological development of the brain, not only with regard to the evolution of the species, but also in terms of the arrangement of brain functions in the early life of each individual human. To consider the physiological basis of language-use is perhaps the obvious place to start.

CHAPTER ONE

SYNTAX AND CIRCUITRY: LANGUAGE, MIND AND BRAIN

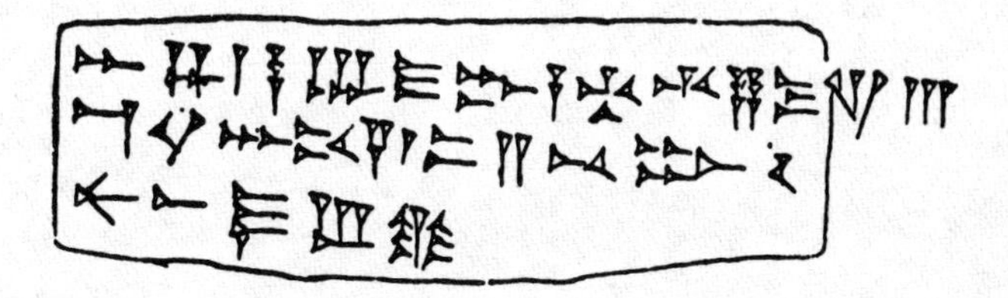

CHAPTER ONE

SYNTAX AND CIRCUITRY: LANGUAGE, MIND AND BRAIN

The unconscious is structured like a language.

Jacques Lacan

Since the middle of the nineteenth century, it has been understood that speaking, writing, signing, reading and hearing language are all activities associated with a particular area of the brain. In the majority of human beings the language centres are located in the left hemisphere. This arrangement is known as 'cerebral dominance'. The correlation of language functions with the left hemisphere holds good for 99 per cent of right-handed people and 66 per cent of left-handed people.

Although the separate components of language (nouns, verbs, and so on) may be the concern of separate areas in this collection of neural structures, research into the behaviour of sensorily deprived patients has shown the extent to which language exists in this section of the brain, irrespective of the medium, visual or aural, through which it must be transmitted. Deaf patients who have sustained damage to the left hemisphere are still able to see the gestures comprising the sign language they are used to, but are incapable of relating the gestures to each other in a way that makes sense.

Damage to a particular part at the back of the left hemisphere (the posterior perisylvian sector) indicates an area that is crucially concerned with the identification of lexical items. Patients with serious lesions in this area may be only partially successful in constructing the words that they need, or they may replace the item they are looking for with a related term ('lorry' for 'tractor' for example). But despite difficulties in selecting items of lexis, particularly proper nouns, such patients do not ordinarily encounter many problems in respect of syntactical organization. By and large, a certain amount of fluency is maintained, the emphases placed are appropriate and relationships between lexical items are established accurately enough.

By contrast, when damage has occurred in the corresponding region at the front of the left hemisphere (the anterior perisylvian sector), patients do experience a struggle with grammar, they omit whole classes of items and their speech is interjected with pauses. Clearly, this area of the brain is employed in general syntactical organization and sentence formation. Unlike patients with posterior lesions, patients with anterior lesions are much more efficient at discriminating between nouns than they are at dealing with verbs.

Many parts of the brain are effectively 'programmed' by the time a human infant is born – the occipital lobe takes care of vision, the motor cortex controls movement – but the largest area that is relatively unprogrammed is the one set aside for what will be developed as language centres. Every language is a pre-arranged system, but the individual brain has to be arranged locally to cope with a particular language or languages (Japanese, Polish, Swahili). Language acquisition is a process involving all the language centres of the brain, anterior and posterior. It now appears that the different language centres are connected and activated by at least two different means. The correlation of lexis and syntax is achieved through the use of different circuits, the cortical and the subcortical. The subcortical circuit is switched on for routine operations, to effect combinations of a kind that have already been learned and have become habitual. The cortical circuit is connected with more original work. It requires greater sophistication and a more conscious engagement with the task of inventing new combinations of language elements. The assimilation of particular linguistic components probably goes through a cortical, then a subcortical stage: to repeat the activity of hearing, reading, speaking or writing any given component does not entail the repeated stimulus of the cortical circuit; after a while, the subcortical takes over. But the transformation of the same component into an equivalent term in a foreign language would lead to the reactivation of the cortical circuit in order to establish a new pattern for future use.

Research points to the likely interaction of three different brain systems in the production and reception of language. The system that is absorbed in the formation of concepts is distinct from that entrusted with the formation of words and sentences, but the two are brought into relation by an obscure mediation system. When language is produced, it is the mediation system that transfers the impulse from the conceptualizing process into a form that can be realized through the language centres. And vice versa, when language is received, the linguistic message bears on the mediation system from another direction, giving it incentive for conceptualization.

More than this, the mediation system itself shows variation linked to a spatial bias. There is a tendency for various kinds of mediation to diverge increasingly on a front-to-back axis:

> Mediation for many general concepts seems to occur at the rear, in the more posterior left temporal regions; mediation for the most specific concepts takes place at the front near the left temporal lobe. We have now seen many patients who have lost their proper nouns, but retain all or most of their common nouns. Their lesions are restricted to the left temporal lobe and medial temporal surface of the brain, sparing the lateral and inferior temporal lobes. The last two, in contrast, are always damaged in the patients with common noun retrieval defects.[1]

Newly developed techniques of positron emission tomography (PET) provide a means of scanning the brain during the performance of several different language functions. The PET scans show that bloodflow is intensified in specific areas, depending on whether the neural structures are engaged in hearing, reading, speaking or conceiving of language items. Moreover, they demonstrate an activation of structures in the

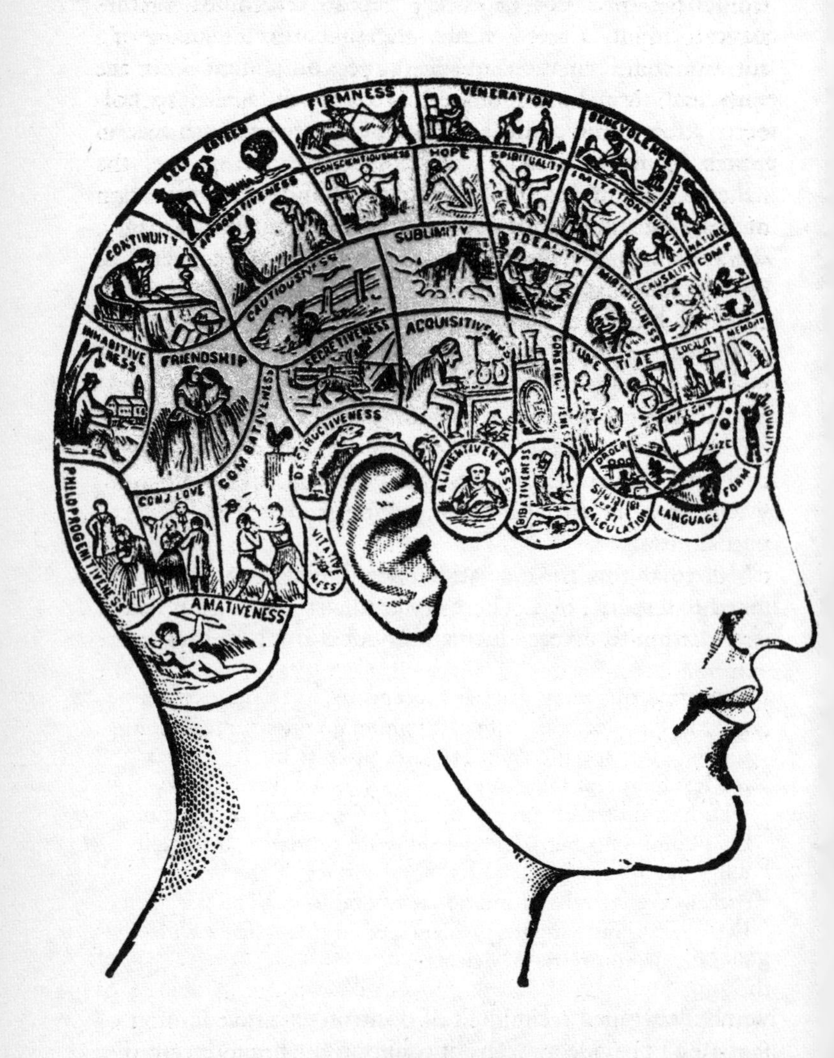

Phrenological head, illustrating a mid-19th century view of the brain, in which smaller areas are allocated to 'language' and 'form' than to 'philoprogenitiveness', or even 'alimentiveness'.

frontal (anterior) cortex during tests in which patients are asked to supply a verb when confronted with the image of a corresponding object or situation (a picture of food elicits the verb 'eat'). Monitoring bloodflow allows the neuropsychologist to establish a topography of language functions in which, broadly speaking, the initiation of language, the management of specific concepts, and the implementation of verb forms, are all associated with front-brain activity, while the visual reception of language, the management of general concepts and the implementation of noun-forms are all associated with back-brain stimulation. Activities related to the aural media (speaking and hearing) are located in the mid-brain system.

There are of course other forms and traditions of research into language disorders that stress social intervention in the structures of the mind rather than biological determination. Psychoanalysis has entered into the most detailed and extensive review of a whole range of damaged and disadvantaged types of language-use, including the language of schizophrenics. The schizophrenic's inability to complete a sentence and thus to relate past and present to future is the extreme case of a deviancy that implies as the boundary for social normalcy a degree of control over language; indeed, it sets a condition for normalcy of the human subject altogether as the successful entry into language itself. Jacques Lacan's famous dictum that the unconscious is structured like a language abbreviates a series of observations on the indispensable role of language structure in the building of every mind.

According to psychoanalytical tradition, schizophrenia is generally characterized by a serious degree of incoherence of thought and language and by an accompanying degree of withdrawal into the self, leading to the overproduction of fantasies. The word 'schizophrenia' itself derives from a Greek verb and noun σχιζω 'split'; φρην 'mind', and indicates what is probably the most fundamental feature of this disease, a splitting of the personality which enables the subject to maintain two separate attitudes towards external, social reality. According to Eugen Bleuler, who first coined the term 'schizophrenia', the disruption of existing mental associations and their rearrangement into other patterns constitute the most decisive effects of this 'splitting' process. Bleuler considered that the first, the disruptive stage of the process was likely to have an organic origin, while the second stage, of rearrangement, was probably the reflection of an adjustment to the change of circumstances – the reflection of an adaptative mechanism in the mind – rather than of an organic disturbance in the brain.

The rearrangement of associations would follow the promptings of the subject's needs and desires, rather than the habitual understanding of objects and their relations given the force and status of rationality by the power of social conventions. In psychoanalytic terms, a normal conception of the reality which exists outside the subject's own psyche is challenged by a 'psychical reality' formed by unconscious desires, or 'affect':

> Everything which opposes the affect is more deeply suppressed than normally, and whatever falls in line with the affect is abnormally facilitated. The result is that an abnormally charged idea cannot even be opposed in thought anymore: the ambitious schizophrenic dreams only of his desires; obstacles simply do not exist for him. In this way, complexes which are joined together by a common affect rather than any logical connection are not only formed, but are also more firmly fixed in the patient. Due to the fact that the associational pathways which join such a complex to other ideas are not used, these associational pathways lose their effectiveness in respect of the more adequate associations. In other words, the effectively charged complex of ideas continues to become isolated and obtains an ever increasing independence.[2]

The language of schizophrenics, then, not only abandons normal sentence structure and habitual ways of making sense with words, it revolves around a new set of private references which it often makes compelling and urgent through sheer insistence and a perverse systematicalness. The private nature of these references is what makes a schizophrenic condition often indistinguishable from a paranoiac one. Freud, in particular, was emphatic in arguing the case for a family resemblance between these two conditions. Paranoid schizophrenics are strikingly prone to delusions of persecution and delusions of grandeur which makes the kind and degree of their divergence from commonly accepted views of external reality particularly revealing; they show how psychical abnormality and linguistic instability can be correlated to form criteria for levels of socialization. The following is an extract from a text dealing with an experience of spiritual election and dated 10–11 October 1976:

> The case or instance of the 10th was all of a slighting to a transfiguration that day coasting hallowed remarkable events of enlightening devastation to audiences proceeding to that ecliptic. The impelling region was rural and dormant dealing in lateral local history. It had although platformed a role significant to warmongering. Idealic territory for the nations involved. Having to border on the French and German come Swiss frontiers. I must have been engaged by some heavily harboured divine influence to enduce a sluice taxing spiritual vexation. The relation of shrines initially was quite, to say the least, impressive, an enignomy that I had ignored until the precedent invasion impeaching my 'will' as character. Appeals to me a miscarriage of justice, bemusing and disruptive in spells of present inverse reliance. Attent to the nucleus of the source. I think in sly terms of staving away the ration of evolution conceived. In thirst of mind in valley and bodily retort. Emploring yearn to assimilate and rejuvenate the ploy as was assigned to in France. Adherent palm that loomed alarm in pending calm to those who slate harm to our drumming charm of Adam complete. A discreet verse coherse to advocate 1986 as the origin of time . . . .[3]

The power of this writing derives from the energy it channels into the attempt to convert a position of disadvantage into one of advantage. The sense of being excluded from society and of isolation is transformed into one of spiritual privilege, and the shame of being unable to meet the conventional demand for semantic coherence is redeemed by giving the lack of clear meaning an almost mystical status. At the same time, there is a simultaneous recognition of how society is likely to judge this linguistic obscurity; at the centre of a passage concerned with justice and impeachment, with the uneasy suspicion that the legal authorities might brand one's behaviour as criminal, the coinage 'enignomy' links enigmatical language with ignominy. The fragmentation of the self has been projected into an anxious monitoring of borders, frontiers and coastlines (even though this last idea is expressed only indirectly in the participle 'coasting'). The separate parts of the self may be represented by different countries (where foreign and incomprehensible languages are spoken); there is an awareness that territory can be invaded and that neighbouring countries can go to war with each other. Mind, body and symbolic territory are made interchangeable, 'in thirst of mind in valley and bodily retort'. Last of all, the process by which 'affectively charged' associations are given unusual independence is illustrated in the enthusiastic use of rhyme, which is allowed to dictate the semantic content. Rhyme is used in order to create harmony between attitudes that the 'splitting' has forced apart; it produces a mechanical reconciliation of 'alarm' and 'calm', of 'harm' and 'charm'.

The 'splitting' of the subject which allows it to maintain two distinct attitudes towards reality, one of recognition and one of withdrawal into a world of private delusions, is both intensified and complicated in those cases where the individual subject is one of a pair of genetic duplicates. Some of the most intriguing empirical data that pose questions about language's relationship with the mind, and the extent to which it is directly 'wired in to the brain', have to do with the special languages of twins. When twins are driven to communicate in a private language whose meanings are understood by none but themselves, it is usually regarded as a safe assumption that the pressures on them to act in this way are largely social and familial ones. However, in cases like that of June and Jennifer Gibbons, the Cardiff twins whose social delinquency spiralled eventually into major arson attacks which led to incarceration in Broadmoor, the genetic duplication that made them nearly identical in external physical appearance extended to an ability to speak in unison, uttering long and varied speeches without any premeditation in a precisely synchronized manner.

To outsiders, however, including members of their own family, the Gibbons twins hardly said anything at all. Paradoxically, their spare time during adolescence was more often than not taken up with an act of communication – the act of writing. They produced long series of essays, stories and poems and even several novels, one of which, *The Pepsi-Cola Addict*, by June Gibbons, was published when the author was only nineteen years old. The language of these productions was, according to Marjorie Wallace, author of a book about the twins, 'primitive in style, but full of energy and sensitivity'.[4] The language they spoke between themselves was almost completely incomprehensible to outsiders; it was a version of English, but dramatically speeded up, with emphases radically misplaced, delivered in a rhythm of short, staccato bursts which made it sound like frenetic birdsong.

The themes of the two girls' writings were uncompromisingly anti-social; their stories were given settings, characters and storylines which emphasized violence, drug-taking and sexual fantasy. This language of indirect communication was one they made a special effort to acquire, enrolling in a creative-writing correspondence course whose exercises they diligently completed. They were anxious to master the conventions of writing, and achieve an 'acceptable' style, precisely in order to write about the wilful and anarchical. On the other hand, the 'unacceptable' obscurity of their spoken language was offset by the formulaic character of much of its content and by the bizarre regimentation of their behaviour during interviews. Above all, the synchronization of their speech is resistant to simple explanation in either neuroscientific or psychoanalytic terms. Indeed, the two horizons of linguistic theory seem to melt into one another, and the theory that language is symbiotic with the mind, producing features that are highly specialized, is divided only by a very thin line from the theory that language is symbiotic with the brain, indicating features that are universal.

The sharp contrast between the use of writing and speech in the double 'splitting' of identical twins, points ultimately to the possibility of a genetic origin for the divergence of these two different forms of language. It is a possibility also evoked by recent Italian research into the impairment of literacy among stroke victims. This research has confirmed that knowledge of the separate components of language is stowed in different parts of the brain, and it suggests that at a very deep level the brain is actually structured according to a pre-existent pattern that corresponds to universally shared aspects of language. Roberto Cubelli of the Ospedale Maggiore in Bologna, has found that patients who have suffered damage to a certain area in the left hemisphere of the brain have retained an understanding of the systematic relations that obtain between consonants although they have lost all means of determining the use or significance of vowels. One patient would write down the name of his home town, Bologna, as 'BLGN'. Even more extraordinary than this demonstration of the way in which the structure of language is organically housed is the revelation that, although some patients could produce both vowels and consonants when speaking, this ability could not be reproduced in writing. The implications of this radical disjunction between writing and speech are potentially very far reaching. Perhaps the majority of scientists and linguists would regard the selectiveness of Cubelli's patients as mysterious. Dr John Marshall, of the Radcliffe Infirmary in Oxford, recognizes that the distinction between vowels and consonants is critical for spoken language, but remarks that 'the main problem is to decide why the distinction should be carried over to written language. At first blush there is no good reason.'

One possibility is that writing serves a fundamentally different purpose from that of speech. This conclusion may seem unlikely from a common-sense point of view, but if so it may be time to revise what passes for common sense. While the historical origins of both writing and speech are inevitably obscure, the history of their relationship is one of the most prominent, and controversial, aspects of language as a cultural phenomenon.

CHAPTER TWO

GRAPHIC EQUALIZER: LANGUAGE IN WRITING AND SPEECH

CHAPTER TWO

GRAPHIC EQUALIZER: LANGUAGE IN WRITING AND SPEECH

> *Polonius*. What do you read, my lord?
> *Hamlet*. Words, words, words.
> *Polonius*. What is the matter, my lord?
> *Hamlet*. Between who?
> *Polonius*. I mean the matter that you read, my lord.

The central Western tradition in the history of thinking about language has to all intents and purposes given precedence to speech over writing. It has been routinely assumed that while speech and writing give rise to and require quite separate systems of signification, the basic *raison d'être* of writing is simply to provide a means of *representing* speech. In a way, writing has been regarded as something of a usurper in the story of language, and the possibility of paying too much attention to it has been seen as an irritating, sometimes even a dangerous, distraction from the real business in hand. 'Writing is foreign to the internal system of language,' says Saussure bluntly. 'Writing obscures our view of the language, writing is not a garment, but a disguise.'[1]

Deeply embedded in Western philosophies of language have been the assumptions that speech came before writing; that writing first developed as a means of pictorial representation; that alphabetic writing established an effective means of representing sounds; and that the superseding of pictographic by alphabetic writing should be judged as evidence of cultural progress. Figures as diversely authoritative as Plato, Aristotle, Rousseau and Saussure have deplored the achievements of writing and regarded its actual cultural primacy over speech as the inversion of a natural order. The only role they have been prepared to assign to writing is in attempting to frame a graphic equivalence to speech: 'words spoken are symbols or signs of affections or impressions of the soul; written words are the signs of words spoken' (Aristotle)[2]; 'a language and its written form constitute two separate systems of signs. The sole reason for the existence of the latter is to represent the former' (Saussure)[3]. Clearly, this long tradition of insisting on the repression of writing could only occur in an alphabetic culture where scripts are designed to correspond closely to the phonological principles of speech; what is written down has an especially close, indeed an imitative, relationship to the sequence of uttered sounds. But this is by no means a universal condition. Moreover, the alphabet must have emerged at a fairly late stage in the history of writing. What is also clear is that the denigration of writing is powerfully motivated. The constant and very animated attempts in the West to give speech a position of supreme importance presupposes that the most vital function language can support is the ability of one individual subject to communicate with another, or with others. This is certainly what is at stake in Socrates' objections to the uses and influence of writing given in Plato's *Phaedrus*: Socrates recounts an Egyptian legend according to which the inventor of writing, the God Theuth (or Thoth), presents his invention to King Thamus, claiming to have devised a 'sure receipt for memory and wisdom'. But Thamus' response is a systematic condemnation of writing and all its works:

> Those who acquire it will cease to exercise their memory and become forgetful; they will rely on writing to bring things to their remembrance by external signs instead of on their own internal resources. What you have discovered is a receipt for recollection, not for memory. And as for wisdom, your pupils will have the reputation for it without the reality: they will receive a quantity of information without proper instruction, and in consequence be thought very knowledgeable when they are for the most part quite ignorant. And because they are

> filled with the conceit of wisdom instead of real wisdom they will be a burden to society.[4]

Thamus anticipates the 'externalization' of knowledge, detached from the experience of individual minds, as a problem implicit in the evolution of writing. Certainly, the reinvention of writing for the purposes of information technology has given a topical urgency to the misgivings of the ancient King of Thebes. Socrates, in his own commentary on his Egyptian tale, tries to count the cost of this externalizing process:

> The fact is, Phaedrus, that writing involves a similar disadvantage to painting. The productions of painting look like living beings, but if you ask them a question they maintain a solemn silence. The same holds true of written words; you might suppose that they understand what they are saying, but if you ask them what they mean by anything they simply return the same answer over and over again. Besides, once a thing is committed to writing it circulates equally among those who understand the subject and those who have no business with it; a writing cannot distinguish between suitable and unsuitable readers. And if it is ill-treated or unfairly abused it always needs its parent to come to its rescue; it is quite incapable of defending or helping itself.[5]

For Socrates, speech is the means by which anyone expresses thoughts and emotions in a way that should be instantly received, challenged, questioned, interpreted and understood by others. It is indissolubly linked to conditions of immediacy and presentness. This kind of insistence may seem natural and uncontroversial to those readers of this book whose linguistic habits were formed in an alphabetical culture. Indeed, the Socratic attitude towards language may meet with general recognition, if not approbation. Why should we be disturbed when writing is expected to efface its own special features as much as possible in the interests of making the content or value of spoken messages as clear as possible? Whether we reflect on it or not, we are nearly all used to the idea that writing should try to be transparent, nothing more nor less than transcription of speech.

Yet the implications of ignoring the potential of writing as a completely independent system of articulation are extremely far-reaching. A number of contemporary philosophers of language, most notably Jacques Derrida, have argued that placing undue stress on the need for the immediate presence of meaning in language-use is out of all proportion, and perhaps even a fatal error; it involves falling into a trap, being tricked into a situation where the issues unfold on an almost inconceivable scale: 'this experience is a lure, but a lure whose necessity has organized an entire structure, or an entire epoch.'[6] Derrida argues that we should not place such a high value on the idea of aiming at fullness or completeness of meaning uttered in speech from moment to moment; this is in any case, strictly speaking, an impossibility, since all words are usually incorporated in more or less extended grammatical structures. Every use of words actually defers meaning; to experience language is to experience delay. Writing only makes this circumstance more vividly obvious than speech, and possesses the means of developing its possibilities with much greater complexity and resonance. Derrida does not want writing and speech to exchange places, in a simple reversal of hierarchical relations; he wants to recover an awareness of language-making as a human faculty that produces systems of signs that operate independently of particular 'substances', whether these substances be written or spoken. Writing and speech are potentially equal means at the disposal of language, and neither should be regarded as enjoying a privileged relationship with it.

Historical data now available offer more comfort to a project like this than to the time-honoured Socratic alternative. Our conventional understanding of the nature of the relationship between speech and writing is brought into question quite simply by considering the variety of scripts used in extinct and living languages. From ancient Egypt to modern-day Beijing, some of the most important centres in the history of civilization have employed glyphs and pictograms that do not have a direct relationship with patterns of sounds, and the link between speech and writing here is only a symbolic one. Particularly fascinating are the variations on the two basic possibilities that have developed with the proliferation of individual cultures. A profound historical change takes place when one culture borrows the pictograms of another in order to employ them in an essentially phonological manner. Something like this has occurred in the case of Japanese, which has borrowed Chinese characters as a vehicle for its own, quite separate, linguistic structures. This is an example of one linguistic code being adapted for the purposes of another in a living system. Of course, there have been many parallels in the growth and decline of languages and cultures now dead. In some cases, the moment of bridging one linguistic code with another represents the occasion of a momentous change in the history of human society. But it is also, quite straightforwardly, one of the most frequent occurrences in the history of language development. The proposition that writing should identify as closely as possible with speech begins to seem completely unrealistic after one has realized just what a rarity the indigenous writing system is: more than nine out of ten of the world's languages have had to turn to other cultures for their scripts.

In fact, the borrowing of scripts is an extremely prominent and, it seems, permanent feature of language development. Some of the most startling and successful examples can be found in quite recent history. A particularly famous case was that of Sequoyah, the Cherokee Indian also known as John Guess, who is credited with being the sole inventor, early in the nineteenth century, of the Cherokee syllabary, or table of syllables. Sequoyah was unable to read English, yet his method was to take letters from the English alphabet in order to use them to represent combinations of sounds in the Cherokee language. The correlation of letters with sounds was established on a basis that was completely arbitrary, and the results must seem absurd to the native speaker of English: the English letter 's', for example, was chosen to render the sound 'du'. Twenty of the characters in Sequoyah's syllabary were borrowed from the English alphabet; the remaining 65 were his own inventions.

The adoption of a script from an alien culture could be taken to reflect a state of national and political crisis; indeed, the fact of adoption may in itself lead to profound complications. In 1928, the Turkish language moved from an Arabic to a Latin script, despite the fact that neither was adequate to reflect the structure of the language. The decision to adopt Latin script and to supplement it with a number of extra features, was evidently a reflection of the Turkish leader Kemal Ataturk's policy of deliberate Europeanization.

The progressive divergence of script and speech is often salient in the evolution of individual languages. Some of the most extravagant discrepancies to be generated in an alphabetical language are those that arise out of the protracted divorce of English spelling and pronunciation. Almost any sample will do to illustrate the maddening inconsistencies between written marks and spoken sounds that English offers to the unsuspecting: *rough, cough, plough, through, dough.*[7] But divergence may stem from historical accidents and be subject to conventional pressures. It is easy to see that divergence might be something that language would move *to*; less easy to imagine divergence as something that language could move *from*. The most significant question to ask in this context is whether the graphic and phonic aspects of language are likely to have been dislocated from each other at the outset?

Recent research on dyslexia in Japan has shown how an inability to interpret logographic writing (writing in which each sign represents a semantic unit) is not necessarily paralleled by an inability to interpret phonographic writing (writing in which each sign represents a unit of sound). This dilemma has cultural resonance in Japan, which makes use of both logographic and phonographic forms of writing. But the fact that the brain processes these two different forms of writing independently of each other exacerbates once more the tensions of the nature/nurture argument. We do not know to what extent specialized dyslexia is an acquired disorder, to what extent it can be given a neurological basis.[8]

The historical point of origin of writing is impossible to determine, although it appears that quite sophisticated writing methods were already in use in Mesopotamia by the fourth millenium BC. Scholarly accounts of subsequent developments have concentrated overwhelmingly on the emergence of, and the cultivation of, the phonographic principle, although in its very beginnings writing may well have had reference to an exclusively graphic means of communication entirely unconnected with speech. Both the ancient Egyptian and the ancient Greek words dealing with the activity of 'writing' were simultaneously employed to express the activity of 'drawing' and, in the case of the Greek, the activities also of 'painting, engraving, scratching and scraping'. One possible starting point for writing has been suggested by the discovery and excavation of boxes of clay tokens from sites in Iran that were occupied from the ninth millenium BC. Interpretation of both the tokens and the boxes has led to the hypothesis that writing in its earliest stages was associated not with literacy but with numeracy, its genesis effected less by speaking than by counting. The tokens were in sets and varied in size and shape; each shape referred to a particular item of merchandise or perhaps a domestic animal. The boxes containing the tokens carried on their lids a pictorial reproduction of the number and nature of the tokens inside; the lid was effectively a clay tablet bearing symbols of symbols. It could not have taken long for the users to realize that these inscriptions were all that was needed to keep a tally of the goods in question and that the tokens themselves could be dispensed with altogether.[9]

But if writing was derived from commerce in this way, it was already locked into a system of substitutions that rendered invalid the idea that *mimesis* (imitation of reality), whether graphic or phonic, was intrinsic to its organization. Several of the tokens and their written equivalents were non-representational, which means their significance was both arbitrary and imposed and they could only be read and understood in context. One explanation for this recourse to arbitrary symbols could be the embargo placed by superstition or religious belief on more direct kinds of representation of particular objects or animals. Writing at the outset may have been subject to restrictions and taboos, prohibitions and censorship.

Surviving myths that enshrine the first encounter with writing, the discovery by a people or a person of its extraordinary capacities and power, often attribute to it supernatural, magical and frequently fearful qualities. It is hardly surprising that a circumstance lost to history and rendered inexplicable should be recovered by the ancient mind as a magical or supernatural event. Writing when first experienced seems to be endowed with an almost limitless power, the power, even, of life and death; and it has continued to evoke the sense of divine sanction. Literacy could literally save the neck of one condemned to death in medieval Europe if he could prove his clerical, divinely sanctioned status by reciting Latin 'neck-verse' (usually the beginning of Psalm 51). The only full and explicit reference to writing in Homer is a cautionary tale, if not a horror story, about the dangers of literacy and the nefarious threat it poses to the illiterate. In Book Six of Homer's *Iliad*, Bellerophon, having rejected the advances of 'the lovely Antea [who] lusted to couple with him', becomes instead a target for resentment, vulnerable to the lies she concocts for her husband King Proetus:

> I wish you'd die, Proetus, if you don't kill Bellerophon!
> Bellerophon's bent on dragging me down with him in lust
> though I fight him all the way!
>   All of it false
> but the King seethed when he heard a tale like that.
> He balked at killing the man – he'd some respect at least –
> but he quickly sent him off to Lycia, gave him tokens,
> murderous signs, scratched in a folded tablet,
> and many of them too, enough to kill a man.
> He told him to show them to Antea's father:
> that would mean his death.[10]

Homer, whose paucity of references to writing in itself suggests that *The Iliad* and *The Odyssey* were composed by an illiterate (or illiterates), here captures the deep-seated mistrust and alarm of a pre-literate society that has seen a future it does not know how to control. Homer (whoever or whatever that name refers to) enters the history of the West on the very threshold of its literacy, and offers therefore a unique bridge between the extremely ancient and the remarkably modern. The time-capsule formulae of oral poetry have preserved through repetition the traditions of thought of a remote antiquity. But when the poems were first committed to writing, probably in the eighth century BC, the linguistic material would have been altered in a simultaneously technological and psychological modernization. As Walter J. Ong has argued, the advent of writing brings with it an entire restructuring of consciousness.[11]

It is instructive to remember how a view of writing which gives it mysterious and even magical properties has lingered in the cultural history of the last two thousand years and has even been linked, paradoxically, to instances of great technical and intellectual innovation. There have always been scripts that no-one knew how to read. The fear and impatience of the pre-literate may always be removed at some future date; but the other kind of apprehension about the secrets of writing looks in the other direction, back to the past where the key to true decipherment has often been lost. In the West, it was the lost meanings of the Egyptian hieroglyphs that sustained, almost to the present day, a romance of supernaturalism that finally guaranteed the superiority of writing over speech.

Egyptian mythology had linked writing with magic in ascribing its origin to the genius of the god Thoth. Once the language ceased to have any living social function, its script was regarded by other cultures as a mysterious code, and the possibility that it embodied supernatural meanings came to dominate European speculation about how it should be interpreted. For many centuries, the single most influential text in the debate over the underlying meaning of Egyptian writing was the fifth-century (AD) *Hieroglyphica* of Horapollo. Although Horapollo was perfectly capable of understanding Egyptian, he was convinced that the established meanings of the written signs were only a part of their function, and argued for a further, secret level of meaning which permitted the use of the hieroglyphs as a set of symbols for nothing less than the Platonic forms themselves. The impact of Horapollo's theories can be gauged by the order of books selected for printing with Gutenberg's movable type: the first was, predictably, the Bible; but the second was the *Hieroglyphica*. Moreover,

The Rosetta Stone, 196 BC. The same inscription appears in Egyptian hieroglyphs, Demotic and Greek.

ironically, the modern decipherment of Egyptian hieroglyphs, made possible by the trilingual texts of the Rosetta Stone, was carried out by Jean-François Champollion, who had previously been a close adherent of Horapollo's ideas. The Stone, which carries a Greek inscription and two Egyptian versions (in hieroglyphic and demotic), was first discovered near Rosetta in Egypt in 1799. Champollion's translation, accomplished in 1822, represented a breakthrough leading directly to comprehension of nearly all the remaining written records of Pharaonic Egypt.

What the history of controversy about the meanings of the hieroglyphs evokes is the possibility that writing relates to language as the projection of an ideal: an ideal that actual human speech used for utilitarian purposes is always going to corrupt. The usual positions are reversed; writing ceases to be regarded as a crude and faulty reproduction of speech, becoming instead a surer means of conveying the paradigmatic, or essential, features of language, those features that ordinary speech must always fail to reflect.

According to the Greek historian Herodotus, the ancient Egyptians employed two separate systems of writing, the 'sacred' and the 'demotic'; but modern research has shown that there were in fact three distinct systems in operation: hieroglyphic (sacred), hieratic (priestly) and demotic (popular). The hieroglyphs were of course pictographic and highly formal; the hieratic was in essence an adaptation and abbreviation of the hieroglyphic style used in the transference of sacred inscriptions from stone to more perishable materials; demotic, which was developed for use in a secular context, used a cursive script, one that could be written with a 'running' hand, moving rapidly from one character to the next and often joining together the separate strokes. The development of the more 'vulgar' scripts has almost everything to do then with a change of writing materials, from the use of dressed stone for the monumental style of the hieroglyphs, to the increasing adoption of papyrus and ink, with a cut reed as a writing implement.

The essential characteristic of logographic writing, in which each separate sign is an attempt to represent an object rather than a word (or even the sound of the word) is that it promotes a legibility that can be achieved without any knowledge of the particular language for which it is used. This facility can be indispensable, as it is for the Chinese who rely on the same characters to make sense of a multitude of separate local dialects. Throughout history, the adaptability of individual languages to a variety of scripts has issued a powerful challenge to Western assumptions of the indissoluble link between writing and speech. In the Ancient World, Assyrian was written down in both cuneiform and the Aramaic alphabet. Later on in Northern Europe, a number of related Germanic languages used both runic and Roman alphabets for hundreds of years. Today, in countries like Malaya and Tanzania, the indigenous language is transcribed by means of both Roman and Arabic alphabets. And in Japan, the number of major writing systems employed is not two, but three.

Bi-graphism, the use of more than one writing system for the same language, has been such a permanent feature in the history of languages, and its use has been so widespread and chronologically extended, that it is perverse to regard the replacement of one writing system with another, and most particularly the replacement of a logographic by a phonographic system, as an infallible mark of progress in the evolution of human culture. From the western point of view, of course, the evolution of human culture has been indistinguishable from the evolution of *homo alphabeticus*, so that the transformations of the Egyptian language might be taken as models for the 'natural' process of shifting towards the interdependence of script and speech. What this process anticipated was arrival at a stage where each hieroglyph no longer stood just for an object but also for the initial consonant of the Egyptian word for that object. This shift of function, on what is called the 'acrophonic' principle, by which a logogram (a written character representing an object, concept or action) may become a phonogram (a written character representing a spoken sound), is commonly seen as preliminary to the invention of syllabaries, in which every written character is given a purely syllabic value.

In some ways, the invention of a syllabary is a much more revolutionary move than the invention of an alphabet, since it makes the great leap from a logographic to a phonographic means of notation, whereas the alphabet has only to refine the method of conveying the phonetic structure of the language. The syllabary offers the advantage of a greatly reduced number of characters needed to deal with any combination of sounds in the given language, although its units of consonants plus vowels still comprise a much larger signary than the average alphabet. Syllabaries have evolved independently in several different parts of the world; the extraordinary thing about the alphabet is that it seems to have been invented only once.

The earliest evidence relates to a Proto-Sinaitic or Proto-Canaanite script carved by miners in the turquoise mines of the Sinai desert. These admittedly fragmentary inscriptions, which date back to 1700 BC, were first recognized as alphabetic because the number of signs the writers had in their repertoire – about 30 – was too limited for the script to be viable in other than alphabetic terms. From this prototype alphabet stemmed most of the major writing systems in use in the world today. Its main descendant in the ancient Near East was Phoenician which was subsequently adapted for use in the Hebrew, Aramaic and Greek scripts; Aramaic became the source for Arabic, while Greek was integral to the formation of both Cyrillic and Roman alphabets.

Another contender for the earliest known alphabetic writing is the Ugaritic script employed in Syria at roughly the same time. Its development was cut short, probably by the awkwardness of its characters, which were cuneiform, resembling the shapes cut by a wedge in soft clay tablets that were subsequently baked. Its suitability to only one medium, and that medium's dependence on the availability of appropriate material, must have inhibited its use and growth. But it is particularly important in providing the earliest known example of an 'abecedary', which is a text that records the number and order of letters in an alphabet. There were 27 in Ugaritic, and their order was the same as in both the later Phoenician and Hebrew alphabets. Intriguingly, Ugaritic was usually written from left to right, as in classical Greek and all subsequent European scripts. The Proto-Sinaitic and Proto-Canaanite scripts had been very unpredictable in this respect, going from left to right, or from right to left, and sometimes even vertically, without any preference. The preferred direction for Phoenician alphabetic writing, which matured around 1100 BC, was from right to left; and the legacy of this can be seen in the habits of all the major Semitic languages of the Middle East today. In the earliest phase of the Greek alphabet, the direction was not fixed.

If we look back at the origins of the alphabet from the vantage point of modern European languages, then the most important of the three main West Semitic versions of alphabetic writing was clearly Phoenician. But the other two variants were of great significance in the cultural and linguistic history of the area. The Aramaic script was derived from the Phoenician, even though the Aramaic language included a number of sounds that the Phoenician script could never successfully represent (this problem was only resolved when the anomalous sounds themselves actually dropped out of use in speech). Aramaic script remained largely unchanged from about the beginning of the first millenium BC to the fall, in the seventh century AD, of the Persian Empire, its last great agent of survival. It diverged from Phoenician early in the first millenium BC, and was separate from Hebrew, the third main variant, even though scripts were occasionally exchanged between the Hebrew and Aramaic languages. Hebrew was also very little changed, probably because of the political and cultural isolation of Israel, even in ancient times. Its use became scarce after the experience of the Babylonian exile in the sixth century BC, and it was replaced by the Aramaic script except in situations and moments of revivalist nationalism, which accounts for its occurrence in some of the Dead Sea Scrolls. Its survival down to the present day is entirely due to its adoption by another ethnic and linguistic group, the Samaritans. The Hebrew language itself was barely used in the last few centuries of the first millenium BC and ceased to be spoken at all at about the time of Christ. Only the establishment of the modern state of Israel has brought its return to life.

Because the earliest alphabets included consonants but excluded vowels they entailed prior knowledge of the language to which they referred for any reader wishing to reproduce the exact combinations of sounds at which the combinations of letters were aimed. To begin with, it was the Hebrew and Aramaic scripts that were used to experiment with the representation of vowel sounds, through the secondary use of the nearest consonants, *h*, *w* and *y*. At first, only the ends of words were subject to this treatment, but then Aramaic began to adapt the new system to cope with internal vowels. It was still only an approximate way of distinguishing between words and syllables whose consonantal structures were the same, since the number of vowels was greater than that of their consonantal 'hosts'. The experiment showed that there was a perceived need for a fully alphabetical system indicating the whole range of consonants and vowels, but that only happened with the emergence of Greek, under circumstances that reward a fairly extended examination.

The great advantage of a true alphabet such as Greek was the possibility it created of transcribing the sounds of any language, not just of the particular language it was first made to serve. This sheer utility and flexibility marks the second great leap forward of alphabet development, after earlier realization of the scope offered by the acrophonic principle. The universal adaptability of the true alphabet argues for its origin in a polyglot milieu where a single, reliable 'language converter' would have been much needed.

According to ancient tradition, the Greeks first learned the art of writing from the Phoenicians. Herodotus provides the fullest as well as the best-known account:

> The Phoenicians who came with Cadmus – amongst whom were the Gephyraei – introduced into Greece, after their settlement in the country, a number of accomplishments, of which the most important was writing, an art till then, I think, unknown to the Greeks. At first they used the same characters as all the other Phoenicians, but as time went on, and they changed their

> language, they also changed the shape of their letters. At that period most of the Greeks in the neighbourhood were Ionians; they were taught these letters by the Phoenicians and adopted them, with a few alterations, for their own use, continuing to refer to them as the Phoenician character – as was only right, as the Phoenicians had introduced them. The Ionians also call paper 'skins' – a survival from antiquity when paper was hard to get, and they did actually use goat and sheep skins to write on. Indeed, even today many foreign peoples use this material. In the temple of Ismenian Apollo at Thebes in Boeotia I have myself seen cauldrons with inscriptions cut on them in Cadmean characters – most of them not very different from the Ionian . . .[12]

The name Cadmus is derived from the semitic root *qdm*, meaning 'the east', so that Cadmus might be a generic description: 'man from the east'. Herodotus pauses over the Ionian practice of referring to paper as if it were 'prepared hide', or ∂ιφθέρα, but of equal interest is the word he takes for granted, βυβλός, since Byblos is the name of the Phoenician port from which Egyptian papyrus was exported throughout the Aegean. The close relationship between Phoenician and 'Ionian' characters is easily perceived: Greek *alpha*, A, and Phoenician *aleph*, ≮, are simply repositioned versions of ∀, the pictograph for a bull's head; *alpha* has no meaning in Greek, but in the West Semitic languages its variants do mean 'bull'.

Despite the generic resonance of the name Cadmus, Herodotus's now-famous formulation, 'Cadmean characters', in focusing on the personal name, appears to reflect a belief that the origin of alphabetic writing in Greek should be attributed to the initiative of a single individual. Remarkable as it may seem, this possibility has genuine support among modern scholars, who base the claim on at least four crucial factors: first, the problem of how to cope with vowels is solved in an original and completely unprecedented manner – the signs for certain Phoenician consonants that were not spoken in Greek were simply borrowed to represent the vowels; secondly, the Greek letter φ (*phi*) is found nowhere in the West Semitic languages but everywhere among the local dialects of Greece, with the sole exception of Cretan; thirdly, the Phoenician names for the sibilants were adopted and reformed by Greek (*zayin* became *san*, while *samekh* became *sigma*), although the original signs they referred to were taken by other Greek letters, *zeta* and *xi*; fourthly, the Phoenician practice of retrograde writing, going from right to left, is replaced in the early phases of Greek by *boustrophedon*, in which the direction of the lines alternates right to left and left to right. (*Boustrophedon* is literally the movement of an ox yoked to a plough that is dragged backwards and forwards across a field.)

After thousands of years of established practice, it is difficult to recover the fluidity of a situation in which not only the order in which the letters are read can undergo change but also the very direction in which the individual letters are pointed. The early Greeks wrote as we would, but also as in a mirror, and even tilted their letters sideways to compose their texts upwards and downwards. This fluidity in the choice of direction, together with an utter carelessness about the divisions between words and larger units such as clauses and sentences, has been seen as evidence of a tendency in early Greek writing to reflect the continuous flow of speech. But on the other hand, it could be pointed out that *boustrophedon* is ideally suited to large-scale public inscriptions by saving the reader from having to walk back to the other end of a building in order to begin each succeeding line.

The earliest Latin scripts of the seventh and sixth centuries BC also used *boustrophedon*, but more often went from right to left. The indecisiveness of early Greek has been taken as a sign that its borrowings from Phoenician must have started at a very early date, long before the first few centuries of the first millenium BC, by which time Phoenician retrograde would have been fixed. The argument would run that different components of the alphabet would have been absorbed and used at different periods of time, so that the whole process of acquiring a full alphabet would have been an extremely long drawn-out one.

This would rule out the single-inventor theory, which

may in any case strike one initially as probably the reflection of a sentimental individualism, even though single inventors are credited with the devising of an extraordinarily high number of scripts: Gothic, Armenian, Glagolitic, Tangut, Korean, Cherokee, Cree, Alaskan, Vai, Mende, Barnum, Apache, Hiao and Dita.[13] But one does not need to hang on to the idea of a single inventor to appreciate how the conditions of a particular culture, in a particular place and time, might favour the sudden emergence and rapid development of a true alphabet. The focus on one individual which the single-inventor theory invites also diminishes the importance of outsiders, of those who bring to the language and culture concerned the necessary means of achieving the revolution at home. As I.J. Gelb, the pioneer historian of writing has observed: 'It is therefore foreign peoples, not bound by local traditions and religions or political interests of an alien group, that are frequently responsible for introducing new and important developments in the history of writing.'[14] In many cultures, writing has remained for long periods the preserve of a scribal elite jealous of its privileges and inimical to change. For this reason, writing systems have rarely been altered from within a milieu dedicated to the strengthening of conventions. The threat posed by the alphabet in particular was its simplicity and the small number of characters it required mastery over; it was easy to learn and therefore opened up the prospect of universal literacy with a concomitant shift in the balance of power. The early Greeks, energetic and independent-minded but also illiterate, were ideally placed to make use of the already existing, incomplete but workable writing system of the Phoenicians.

The twin points of contact between the two cultures are likely to have been the Greek trading post of Al Mina, in northern Syria, and the island of Euboea. Euboean pottery has been found among the earliest levels of settlement in Al Mina, where there would have been a Phoenician majority, while excavations at Lefkandi in Euboea have produced Phoenician artifacts dating back to a period when the rest of Greece appears to have been completely cut off from contact with the east. The Euboean alphabet was almost certainly the earliest Greek alphabet but, despite being phased out in Greece itself, its influence has extended perhaps even further than that of the classical Greek script, Ionic. From Euboean colonies in Italy, this earliest alphabet was adopted by Etruscans and later modified by the Romans who introduced it to all those regions of the Empire where Greek was not already in use. The supremacy of Ionic among the local dialects of Greece was only confirmed through its official adoption by Athens in 403 BC. The reasons for its adoption, which incidentally settled the issue of direction, since the Ionic habit was to go from left to right, are extremely revealing and may throw some light back onto the reasons and timing of Greek's original adoption of the alphabet itself.

Although Athens, with its democratic system of government, made copious use of writing for official purposes and produced huge quantities of public records and inscriptions, the Attic dialect was supplanted by that of a state greatly inferior in political and military terms. The only claim to superiority the Ionians could realistically be allowed was that of cultural pre-eminence, for theirs was the language of Homer, recognized everywhere as the most important poet of the Greek world. In sharp contrast to those Bronze Age cultures in which writing itself had developed, where the primary function of the new invention was to record and facilitate economic transactions, the Greeks regarded their alphabet first of all as the means by which literature could be written down. And there are many signs that this was the very motive force behind the creation of the Greek alphabet in the first place.

The corpus of Greek inscriptions from the Archaic period is very large and many of them consist of the merest fragments, but it is intriguing that a majority of the longer inscriptions from the early period of the eighth to the seventh century BC have the formal characteristics of literary texts. One of the very oldest examples of alphabetic writing is found on the cup of Nestor, so called because it resembles the cup, described by Homer, which Nestor,

> The old King brought from home,
> studded with golden nails, fitted with handles,
> four all told and two doves perched on each,
> heads bending to drink and made of solid gold
> and twin supports ran down to form the base.
> An average man would strain to lift it off the table
> when it was full, but Nestor, old as he was,
> could hoist it up with ease.[15]

The cup, which survives, was found in a cremation burial at the Euboean colony of Pithekoussai, an island off the west coast of Italy. It is inscribed with three lines of verse: 'I am the cup of Nestor, a joy to drink from./Whoever drinks this cup, straightway that man/the desire of beautiful-crowned Aphrodite will seize.' In the original Greek, the lines are unmistakeably composed in a poetic metre, and this results in a remarkable set of circumstances: one of the oldest alphabetical inscriptions is not only Euboean, it is also composed as literature and comprises a literary allusion: the allusion is to a passage in the *Iliad* of Homer, the cultural authority of the archaic and classical Greek world.

Research into other 'long' inscriptions of the period, such as that on the 'Dipylon oinochoe', an Attic geometric vase, or the obscene graffiti of Mesavouno on the island of Thera, shows a pattern emerging that is reflected in a very wide spread of writings found on sites all over the Greek world from Pithekoussai and Cumae in the west to Rhodes and Smyrna in the east: an absence of anything with a public or economic character and a prevalence of literary writing, nearly always in hexameter (a verse line of six 'feet'[16]) and often with reference to the hedonistic milieu of the symposium, a literary party that mixed drinking with intellectual conversation. Herodotus's account of the import of 'Cadmean characters' goes on to record three ancient inscriptions on cauldrons in the temple of Ismenian Apollo at Thebes:

> There were three of those cauldrons; one was inscribed: 'Amphitryon dedicated me from the spoils of the Teleboae', and would date from about the time of Laius, son of Labdacus, grandson of Polydorus and great-grandson of Cadmus. Another had an inscription of two hexameter verses:

> Scaeus the boxer, victorious in the contest,
> Gave me to Apollo, the archer God, a lovely offering.

This might be Scaeus the son of Hippocöon; and the bowl, if it was dedicated by him and not by someone else of the same name, would be contemporary with Laius's son Oedipus. The third was also inscribed in hexameter:

> Laodamus, while he reigned, dedicated this cauldron
> To the good archer Apollo – a lovely offering.[17]

Two out of three of the inscriptions are in hexameter – Herodotus's sample is statistically an almost exact reflection of the distribution of hexametrical and non-hexametrical finds in the archaeological record. The popularity of hexameter shows how the alphabet was seized as a means of writing down literature and making it available to a much wider audience than the tiny aristocratic courts in which *aoidoi*, or oral poets, had held the monopoly on the traditional modes of verse composition. With the development of the alphabet came a tremendous expansion of thematic material in Greek art, reflecting a wider awareness of the details of Greek legend and particularly of Homer. The *aoidoi* were replaced by the *rhapsodoi*, reciters of written poetry, who would perform to the general public rather than to elite gatherings. The name *rhapsodos* was most commonly given to those who could earn a living by reciting the poems of Homer.[18]

The great paradox is that alphabetic culture, which has been largely responsible for the chronic desire to fuse writing and speech and make one the instrument of the other, should have begun with an apparent determination to emancipate writing from its inferior status. Socrates complained that writing circulated equally among those who understood the subject and those 'who had no business with it'. The inventor or inventors of the alphabet might well have agreed, adding that the whole point of the enterprise was to make language the business of everybody; gaining power over language meant a redistribution of power. The difference between the situations of the *aoidoi* and the *rhapsodoi* was a profound one. Writing provided a different way of relating to history and tradition, on different terms. Ultimately it begged the question whether language was not to be thought of as concerned with *communication* above all else, but with a form of *memory* (not the sort that Socrates or Plato approved of). Once language has been established, it is of course always bound up in conditions of communication, but that does not mean that the prototypical act of communication necessarily involves a speaker and listener who are immediately present to one another. We should rather think in terms of the significance of communications that take place between persons separated in both space and time. To take this further and to put it more dramatically, the secret purpose of language may not be to further communication between the living and the living, but between the living and the dead.

CHAPTER THREE

THE CURSE FROM BABEL: THE DISTRIBUTION OF LANGUAGES

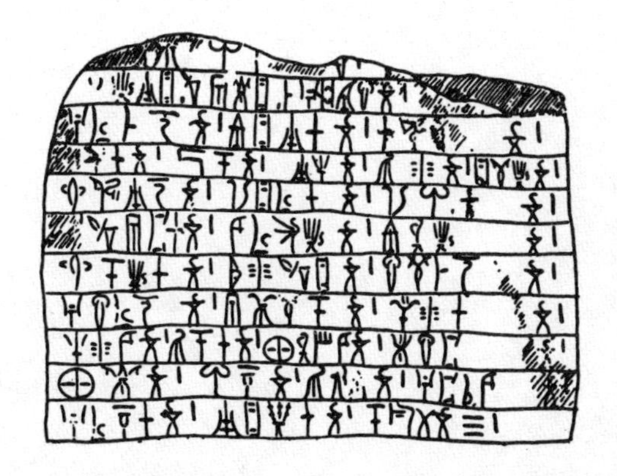

CHAPTER THREE

THE CURSE FROM BABEL: THE DISTRIBUTION OF LANGUAGES

> The same territory with a different name makes no more sense than a different state with the same name.
>
> Stephen Rodefer[1]

In the long perspective of language-use, there must have been innumerable factors determining the way in which different languages have been distributed across the globe. There can be no simple form of explanation for the predominance of particular languages in particular areas. However, certain kinds of evidence – archaeological, anthropological, linguistic – can be drawn together in the effort to unveil how it was, and why, certain languages spread into certain areas and not others.

Perhaps the greatest single challenge to such an account is Indo-European, a family of languages now spoken by half the world's population. Linguists calculate that it has taken no more than six thousand years for this situation to develop, although questions about the geographical and historical origins of Indo-European are among the most fiercely contested issues of linguistic prehistory. The gradual realization that such an entity as Indo-European might exist, and that the various Indo-European languages might all have stemmed from a single Proto-Indo-European language, is the subject of a narrative of discovery equally fascinating in its own right as the reconstructed history of the development of Indo-European itself. The first man to coin the phrase was Thomas Young, in 1813, but the most famous expression of the concept behind the phrase was delivered by Sir William Jones, Chief Justice of India and founder of the Royal Asiatic Society, who in 1796 included the following claim in a discourse on Indian culture:

> The Sanskrit language, whatever may be its antiquity, is of wonderful structure; more perfect than the Greek, more copious than the Latin, and more exquisitely refined than either; yet bearing to both of them a stronger affinity, both in the roots of verbs and in the forms of grammar, than could have been produced by accident; so strong that no philologer could examine all the three without believing them to have sprung from some common source, which, perhaps, no longer exists. There is a similar reason, though not quite so forcible, for supposing that both the Gothic and Celtic, though blended with a different idiom, had the same origin with the Sanskrit; and the old Persian might be added to the same family.[2]

Sir William Jones's projections were to prove remarkably accurate, although many other languages might be added to his final list, including the Slavonic and Baltic groups, and several languages now extinct. Throughout the nineteenth century, the model most readily employed to represent the interrelationships of these various languages was an evolutionary one, established by August Schleicher (1821–68). Schleicher adopted the model of the family tree and portrayed the development of languages with the help of terms used to account for the divergence of genera and species in natural history. It was an effective model, but was not without its problems. For one thing, it tended to explain the growth of linguistic differences in terms of the movements of peoples, and thus cemented a controversial link between language and race. Secondly, its coherence was derived from the assumption that languages always *diverged* with the passing of time, and never *converged*, whereas the historical record shows that the latter has often been the case: English, for example, has experienced convergence with French during the last one thousand years, although like several other Northern European languages, it started by diverging from an emphatically Germanic original.

In the later nineteenth century, the family tree model was rivalled, although never completely supplanted, by an alternative model proposed by Johannes Schmidt (1843–1901). Schmidt advanced a wave theory, according to which linguistic relations within the Indo-European family could be portrayed as a series of overlapping circles. Each circle represented a geographical area, with linguistic influence spreading out in waves from the centre of each circle, sometimes petering out in conditions of geographical separation from other languages, sometimes overlapping with other waves where convergence was the rule. The wave theory allowed for both divergence and convergence, but it had no chronological dimension; it did not indicate *when* languages made or lost contact: during what historical phase they either came closer together or moved off into linguistic remoteness and isolation.

Many of the data that have to be confronted in studying the distribution of languages cannot be incorporated into any of the available models. Or at least, the explanations supplied by the models are less than convincing. One such language is Tocharian. Although it is spoken only on the very borders of China, it has extremely close links with several European languages. Moreover, scholars are generally agreed that it has a number of extremely archaic features, making it closer to the notional Proto-Indo-European than all other groups except for Celtic, Italic, Hittite and Phrygian (the last two being ancient languages spoken mainly in Asia Minor). Most extraordinary of all, Tocharian disrupts the so-called *centum/satem* pattern. This distinction, between the Latin and Iranian words for a hundred, in dividing languages into those which begin their word for a hundred with a 'k' sound, and those which use an 's' sound, arranges the Indo-European family into two main groups, along a rather unsteady axis dividing west from east, with United Asia Minor as a notional median point. Clearly, Tocharian does not conform to this arrangement. It is a language which, despite its geographical remoteness, seems to have diverged less than others closer to the supposed Indo-European homeland (somewhere between Anatolia and the West Russian steppe): it displays many effects we have come to associate with convergence, even though it is dislocated several thousand miles from languages with which it has most in common.

A greater variety of models is needed, and a greater flexibility of response to the conundrums of language distribution. Archaeology has come to play an increasingly important part in the assessment of Indo-European origins and development; recent work, particularly that by Colin Renfrew, has added to the research of palaeolinguistics a systematic reduction of the possibilities implied by the material evidence.[3] Renfrew has identified four critical pressures affecting the pattern of distribution. The first emerges from a sociological account of demographic pressure in respect of population expansion, technological innovation and subsistence requirements. A second depends on the analysis of power struggles between ethnic groups, periodically resulting in the establishment of dominant élites. Elite dominance in political, social and cultural terms does not always entail linguistic dominance, however; the history of English provides one major example of a language that has survived the experience of élite dominance. A third pressure is referred to as 'system collapse'. This occurs when a centrally organized society develops a specialized economy unable to cope with crises such as bad harvests; the collapse of the system allows takeover by neighbouring linguistic groups. The fourth pressure stems from the growing importance of commerce and the rise of international trade in the ancient world; this would have precipitated the formation of a *lingua franca*. In every case, whichever pressure, or combination of pressures, is operating, a scenario is to be imagined in which the society in question has to go through a period of bilingualism. For much of its history, the Indo-European family of languages has been involved in bilingual relationships and the culturally challenging experience of language shift.

One aspect of language diffusion underplayed by Renfrew involves recognition of the importance of religious cults and ideologies and how they are transmitted from one culture to another. Renfrew places little weight on such factors because they are stressed by palaeolinguists he distrusts for their reliance on deduction rather than material remains. Palaeolinguists attempt to reconstruct ancient cultures using lexical evidence; such reconstructions have a limited validity, but even allowing for their limitations, the conclusions arrived at can be extremely revealing. And if one puts the case of Indo-European alongside that of other language groups, such as Finno-Ugric and Semitic, it is hard to maintain that belief systems do not sometimes play a crucial role in the history of language distribution. Concentrating on religion, myth and ideology as a focus for studying the linguistic relations of different cultures has always been at the centre of scholarly attempts to fathom Indo-European origins, even before it was realized what an Indo-European origin was or might be. Joseph Scaliger, in the sixteenth century, divided the languages of Europe into four groups, according to the words given to the concept 'god'; the Romance words for god (e.g. Italian, *dio*; French, *dieu*) all derived from the Latin *deus*; the Germanic appellations were all variations of *Gott* or *god*; the Slavonic name was always a version of *bog*; while the Greek *theos* was, it is now clear, the source for *deus* and all its descendants. In the eighteenth century, the separation of the European languages from each other was understood with reference to the biblical myth of Noah's sons; the dispersing tribes of Shem, Ham and Japhet were held to account for the distinction between Semitic (Jewish, Arabic), Hamitic (Egyptian, Cushite) and Japhetic (the remaining) languages.[4]

The ancient perception of the origins of language was governed by the use of myth. Herodotus records an Egyptian legend about an attempt to discover the proto-language by practical, experimental means. In a curious anticipation of later *causes célèbres* such as Kaspar Hauser, or the Wild boy of Aveyron, the story describes how the seventh-century BC Egyptian King Psammetichus made preparations for one of his shepherds to rear the two newly born infants in strict linguistic isolation:

> All these arrangements were made by Psammetichus
> because he wished to find out what word the children

> would first utter, once they had grown out of their meaningless baby-talk. The plan succeeded; two years later the shepherd, who during that time had done everything he had been told to do, happened one day to open the door of the cottage and go in, when both children, running up to him with hands outstretched, pronounced the word 'becos'. The first time this occurred the shepherd made no mention of it; but later, when he found that every time he visited the children to attend to their needs the same word was constantly repeated by them, he informed his master. Psammetichus ordered the children to be brought to him, and when he himself heard them say 'becos' he determined to find out to what language the word belonged. His inquiries revealed that it was the Phrygian for 'bread', and in consideration of this the Egyptians yielded their claims and admitted the superior antiquity of the Phrygians.[5]

The most convincing element of the story is the information at the end which registers how the Egyptian sense of superiority gives way, unusually, to Phrygian claims for greater antiquity. This very uncharacteristic downgrading of Egyptian status might reflect an historically rooted perception of linguistic relations in the ancient Near East. An archaeologist could point to the remarkable circumstance of a myth of origins being folded around what appears to be a recognition of the importance of material factors in the spread of language use. If the first word is the word for 'bread', this might suggest the priority of demographic over other pressures behind the various advancing waves of linguistic influence. Phrygian was actually on the move from about 1200 BC to the time of Psammetichus, spreading its influence from Macedonia down through Asia Minor. Among those languages on the retreat before its wave of advance were Hittite, Luwian and Palaic, comprising the Anatolian group. These are the earliest Indo-European languages for which contemporary written evidence survives. There is ample documentation of Hittite, in particular, in the form of palace records from the imperial centre at Boghazköy. With the increasing use of Phrygian in west and central Anatolia, and of Armenian in the east, Hittite, Luwian and Palaic were all to become quite rapidly extinct.

Further to the east, the earliest testimony for the Indo-Aryan group of languages survives either in ancient religious texts or in the form of references to religious names. The predecessor of Sanskrit, Old Indic, can be glimpsed in the *Vedas*, religious texts that were set down in the sixth century BC although they are extremely archaic in form and probably existed in oral versions well before 1000 BC. The characteristics of an early Indo-European society and culture that can be elicited from the *Vedas* find parallels in the written and archaeological evidence associated with other areas that fall within the orbit of Indo-European influence, north, south, east and west. The *Vedas* celebrate the displacement of one, indigenous, culture by another that is highly mobile, perhaps nomadic, definitely non-urban and illiterate; its political structures are simple, focusing on a king whose responsibilities are both martial and ritual; its economy is essentially pastoral, with an emphasis on the exchange of cattle; most important of all, perhaps, it relies upon superior skills at horse- and chariot-riding. In rudimentary fashion, this basic profile recurs throughout the Indo-European world.

The very earliest written examples of an Indo-Aryan language are in the language of the Mitanni, a people who must have inhabited an area on the western borders of Hittite influence. Intriguingly, the evidence that is still extant gives prominence in equal measure to both religious and material cultures. In one text, a treaty between the Hittites and the Mitanni, which must have been drawn up at some point between 1600 and 1400 BC, the King of the Mitanni solemnizes his oath by appealing to four deities whose names are virtually indistinguishable from those of their counterparts in ancient (and present-day) Indian culture:

Mitanni	Indic
Mi - it - ra	*Mitra*
Aru - na	*Varuna*
In - da - ra	*Indra*
Na - sa - at - kya	*Nasatya*

The other Mitanni text is embedded deep inside a Hittite document, on horse-training and chariotry, whose author is identified as Kikkuli the Mittani. In this discourse on one of the most fundamental and characteristic aspects of Indo-European culture, Kikkuli employs numerals which are again astonishingly close to their Indic equivalents. But there are other, clearly non-Indo-European, elements of the Mitanni language borrowed from the Hurrians, earlier occupants of the same area held by the Mitanni in the middle of the second millenium BC. The fact that the Indic elements of Mittani are associated with deities, horse-riding and chariotry is enough to evoke a scenario of élite dominance, with an Indic élite, equipped with superior military technology and skills, imposing its religious culture on a Hurrian-speaking indigenous population.

The other major language group in this eastern sphere of the Indo-European continuum is Iranian. The earliest precursor to modern Iranian languages for which written evidence survives was Avestan, so called because the oldest texts comprised a body of religious literature named the *Avesta*. As with the *Vedas*, the earliest samples, a series of hymns entitled *Gathas*, were archaic in character; their authorship was ascribed to Zarathustra, an attribution that has no small significance. The *Gathas* supply less detail of a sociocultural kind than the *Vedas*, although they presuppose a rural rather than an urban locus, with an emphasis on stock-breeding. There is no allowance for a complex political structure; the context for power relations is limited to arrangements for the family, village and tribe. Once again, examination of the names for deities uncovers the bare outline of a possible account of linguistic relations, this time between prehistoric Indic and prehistoric Iranian. The Indic word for god, *deva*, was adopted by Iranian as *daeva*, but simultaneously demoted in being used to refer not to 'god', but to 'demon'. This sharp twist given to the meaning of the word is one index of the intimate connection that is often sustained between the spread of religious cults and the distribution of languages. The incoming religion of Zoroastrianism exerted its influence through the denigration of the older Indian gods;

the new religion was carried by an influx of Iranian-speaking peoples from the north which divided the indigenous Indic-speaking population into separate western (Mitanni) and eastern (Indian) branches. It is highly significant that the earliest Iranian texts are the sacred hymns of this new religion, supposedly authored by Zarathustra himself. The link between literary and cultural supremacy has aready been made in investigating the origins of the Greek alphabet – in the absence of exclusively religious texts, Homer provided the nearest equivalent to a sacred book for archaic Greek culture. The superimposition of language and cult in the process of cultural diffusion has become more and more pronounced in the era of the book, and the relationship between the two factors has become more profound; it has been of absolutely seminal importance in the distribution of Arabic, for example, and is of explosive significance in the rivalry between Greek and the indigenous languages of Palestine at the time of the early Christian church.

Greek became one of the most important of the Indo-European languages, although its earliest speakers were extremely receptive to elements of the pre-Greek culture they encountered on first migrating into the area we have come to identify with the Greeks since archaic and classical times. It is hardly surprising that the first Indo-European settlers in this part of the Mediterranean should have adopted local names for flora and fauna that were probably quite unknown in the original homeland further north; but it is revealing that several names of mythical heroes and deities appear to be of non-Indo-European origin. These include: Aphrodite (goddess of love), Athene (goddess of wisdom), Hera (queen of the gods), Hermes (messenger of the gods), Achilles (the principal Greek warrior in the siege of Troy), Odysseus (the wandering protagonist of *The Odyssey*) and Theseus (the ancestral hero of Athens who outwitted the Minotaur). The first attempts at writing Greek employed a local syllabary originally designed for a non-Indo-European language. Linear B, although not ideally suited to Greek, is the script in which the oldest examples of proto-Greek have been found; extensive archives of clay tablets containing palace records in Linear B have been excavated from sites such as Knossos and Phaistos on Minoan Crete, and from the Mycenaean Greek mainland, notably at Pylos, Argos and Mycenae itself. Linear B was employed by these palace regimes throughout the early Greek world in the second half of the second millenium BC; Linear A is the script it most closely resembles, although Linear A was used exclusively in conjunction with another language that was not Greek at all, and that has still not been deciphered. The military superiority of the Greeks does not seem to have been accompanied at this early stage by a corresponding ideological aggressiveness; and the slightly later phenomenon of Homer (early first millenium BC) marks the extent to which issues of cultural supremacy in the Greek world had a robustly secular, rather than fanatically religious, character.

The other major languages in this area at this time were Thracian and Illyrian. They were predominant in the Balkans, where they were associated with extremely large and powerful ethnic groups. According to Herodotus, the Thracians were the second most populous nation in the world (after the Indians); but this has not prevented their language from becoming utterly extinct. Illyrian has suffered a similar fate, although it is just possible that a modern derivative from it exists in the shape of Albanian. The erosion of these languages might not be entirely unrelated to the military fortunes of the Thracians and Illyrians. Homer puts them on the losing side in *The Iliad*, and it may be that the gradual extension of Greek cultural hegemony throughout the Aegean and the Balkans involved a process that is partly reflected in Homer's semi-historical, semi-mythical account of military setbacks for the Trojan allies.

North of the Balkans were situated the homelands for two of the most important Indo-European language groups, Slavic and Baltic. Hydronymy (the analysis of river names) suggests that the limits of Slavic territory were the Vistula in the West and the Dnieper in the East. This was roughly the area claimed by Herodotus to have been occupied by the Scythians; it was either from the Scythians or the Sarmatians – an Iranian-speaking people – that the

Slavic languages inherited their common words for 'god', 'holy' and 'paradise'. There is relatively little divergence among some of the Slavic languages (Russian, Polish, Ukrainian, Czech, Slovak) since the common Slavic language did not start to divide up into its modern descendants until after 400 AD.

North of the Slavs were the Balts, now confined to Lithuania and Latvia although their homeland once occupied an area six times larger, extending into the region that became known historically as Prussia. Old Prussian was in fact the chief Baltic language and only became extinct as late as 1700 AD. According to Herodotus, the reason for the contraction of the Baltic homeland was a plague of snakes, and it is remarkable that the cultic practices of pagan Lithuania centred on the indigenous green snake. Each household was supposed to care for its own snake, and when the area was Christianized by the Germans in the early middle ages, this was only accomplished by a widespread destruction of snakes, which the Germans collected and burned in great public bonfires. Herodotus also mentions another item of folklore, the superstition that 'once a year every Neurian turns into a wolf for a day or two, and then turns back into a man again.' Whatever the origin of this fantasy, it is clearly of great antiquity and centres on a word which in Lithuanian has extremely ancient roots; the Lithuanian word for the noun 'wolf' is almost identical in declension to that of its Sanskrit equivalent. The three thousand years that separate the earliest examples of Sanskrit from present-day Lithuanian convey how archaic the modern Baltic languages are. Paradoxically, the oldest Baltic writings are no earlier than sixteenth century; they are religious texts again, including Lutheran catechisms. Yet a comparison of the wording for the same proverb in different Indo-European languages indicates the structural antiquity of Lithuanian:

ENGLISH: 'God gave teeth, God will give bread'
LATIN: 'Deus dedit dentes, Deus dabit panem'
SANSKRIT: 'Devas adadat datis, Devas dat dhanas'
LITHUANIAN: 'Dievas dave dantis, Dievas duos duonos'

The remaining language-groups in the Indo-European family are Germanic, Italic and Celtic. The first two are the largest groups in the family and the third is one of the smallest. In excess of 600 million people speak a North or West Germanic language (English, German, Dutch, Afrikaans, Danish, Swedish, Norwegian, Icelandic); roughly 550 million people speak a version of Italic (French, Spanish, Portuguese, Italian, Romanian). The number of Celtic speakers is now three million at most. And yet in the prehistoric era, Celtic-speaking territories extended over western, central *and* eastern Europe. The steady push southwards and westwards of the Germans (a tribe located by Tacitus, in around 98 AD, between the Oder and Rhine) and the inexorable growth of the Roman empire, eradicated Celtic as a continental language and restricted it to the insular 'fringe' of Ireland, Brittany, Scotland, Wales and Cornwall. The earliest identifiable form of Germanic was Gothic, for which a single inventor, Bishop Wulfilas, devised an alphabet, based on Greek. Gothic was still being spoken as late as in the sixteenth century, far to the east in the Crimea. The emergence of Italic entailed the displacement of a host of indigenous languages from the Italian peninsula, early in the first millenium BC. The most significant of these was Etruscan, which appears unrelated to any other known language, although it is strikingly well attested to, over 10,000 inscriptions having been recovered so far.

The manner of distribution of the various groups of languages within the Indo-European family has been anything but uniform, involving a mixture of the factors identified by Renfrew with a number of others as well. Archaeology has been able to confirm in many instances how a combination – in varying proportions – of demographic pressure, the use of a *lingua franca*, élite dominance, system collapse and the spread of religious cults, has governed the pattern of interactions between Indo-European and non-Indo-European languages. But any attempt to retrace the path taken by diverging languages back to a common original can only reach so far before it has to abandon reliance on archaological remains and resort to the languages themselves for evidence of the social structure and culture of those peoples who introduced language shifts throughout the Indo-European world. It is possible to reconstruct part of the history of distribution throughout territories occupied by Indo-European, by monitoring the nuances of individual languages with regard to a basic cultural lexicon found in many of them. By collecting the lexical similarities between languages that have never been geographically adjacent, and so have not been prone to convergence, it becomes possible to establish a core vocabulary of terms giving an outline of the physical and conceptual world of the earliest speakers of Indo-European. This vocabulary has been called the 'proto-lexicon', and its most revealing items concern the religious and ideological profile of this prehistoric society whose language has affected the formation of many of the major cultures existing today.

Physically, the proto-Indo-European world was extensively forested, with the most widespread names of trees including those for birch, willow, ash and elm. The fauna indicated in the proto-lexicon include the forest-dwellers, bear, deer and elk, as well as the river users, otter and beaver. Domesticated animals were numerous; the proto-Indo-Europeans had experience of agriculture, but clearly their economy centred on stock-breeding, mainly of cattle, but also of sheep, goats and pigs. By far the most important animal, in practical and cultural terms, was the horse; it provided the only animal name to be incorporated into early Indo-European personal names; it was occasionally revered – archaeologists have uncovered burial sites where horses were interred with great ceremony. The horse facilitated a pastoral and semi-nomadic existence and, as has already been pointed out, it gave the Indo-Europeans their military edge.

The social relations disclosed by the proto-lexicon are highly specific. Curiously, there is virtually no consistency among the names for husband and wife throughout the Indo-European world, although there is fairly widespread agreement on a name for widow, for which the proto-Indo-European projection is *widhewa*. There is similarly no source word for marriage, although there is sufficient correspondence among several languages to propose a notional proto-Indo-European verb *wedh*, meaning 'to lead home'. The only word connected with marriage that we know of presents the ceremony from the point of view of the groom, leading the bride from her father's house to that of his own family. This is our first indication of the extent to which social customs among the proto-Indo-Europeans had a strongly patriarchal character. Perhaps the most singular feature of the kinship relations implied by the proto-lexicon stresses the importance of the relationship between uncles and nephews, specifically, maternal uncles and sister's sons. According to Tacitus, the ancient Germans considered the bond between maternal uncle and sister's son to be as socially valuable as that between father and son. The need for the sister's son to rely on his mother's brothers for advice and support might suggest a degree of alienation from the father, who is cast in a primarily authoritarian role.

Indo-European society as a whole was quite strictly hierarchical, and in this respect there are extensive correspondences between various languages and cultures which reveal a basically tripartite structure. Broadly speaking, the Indo-European community was divided into three unequal groups: priests, warriors and herder-cultivators. The cultural lexicons of the early Indians, Iranians, Greeks and Romans all reproduce this triadic arrangement, and it appears to be reflected in the religious and legal formulae and in the myths of numerous other cultures. The treaty between the Hittites and the Mitanni already referred to includes the invocation to different Indic gods; each is associated with one of the three estates of Indo-European society. Mitra and Varuna represent the executive and priestly aspects of sovereignty; Indra is the god of war; the Nasatyas comprise one among many Indo-European pairs of twins linked to the care of horses. This triangulation of deities aligned with the three estates, or functions, within society, conforms to a pattern found throughout the Indo-European world. The original trio of Roman gods was composed of Jupiter, Mars and Quirinus (the name given to Romulus the mythical founder of Rome, after his deification). The Greek myth of the judgement of Paris actually draws attention to the different properties of the three goddesses Hera, Athene and Aphrodite (Hera was Zeus's queen; Athene was often depicted as a warrior; Aphrodite's connection with fertility linked her to the cultivation of the earth). Similar distinctions appear to have governed the shape of ancient Greek and Iranian medical practices, with three different kinds of treatment being prescribed according to the nature of the illness: spells to cure sores, incisions to deal with wounds, and herbs and potions to resist exhaustion. Even human sacrifice was subject to these or similar criteria. In some Germanic and Celtic traditions, sacrifice to a sovereign deity meant death by hanging; sacrifice to the gods of war was accomplished by the knife or by fire; an offering to the goddess of fertility was achieved by drowning the victim.

A number of mythical accounts preserved in the early writings of several of those societies revolve around the inherent divisiveness of this tripartite structure. Indian, Norse and Roman legends tell of a war between the different strata of society, and attempt to give a semi-historical justification of the domination of the lower orders of society by the victors. Other narratives portray the hierarchy as God-given, or show how the position of privilege and pre-eminence has been obtained by merit. One particularly intriguing illustration of this approach is provided by Herodotus, who recounts the myth purveyed by the Scythians about their own origins:

> The first man to live in their country, which before his birth was uninhabited, was a certain Targitaus . . . . Targitaus had three sons, Lipoxais, Arpoxais, and Colaxais, the youngest; and during their reign in Scythia there fell from the sky a golden plough, a golden yoke, a golden battle-axe, and a golden cup. The eldest of the three was the first to see these treasures, and as he went to pick them up the gold caught fire. At this he retired, and the second of the brothers approached; but the gold caught fire and blazed, just as before. Lastly, when the two elder brothers had been kept off by the flames, the youngest came along,

> and this time the fire went out, so that he was able to pick up the golden implements and carry them home. The elder brothers accepted this as a sign from heaven and made over the whole kingdom to Colaxais.[6]

The golden objects can be divided into three categories: the golden cup may evoke ritual usage by a priestly class; the golden battle-axe clearly suggests the occupation of warrior; the golden plough and yoke refer to cultivation of the land. It is important that this classification of the objects has divine sanction, and even more important that the elder brothers recognize and concede the superior claim to kingship of their younger sibling, Colaxais. Such myths of origin, which stress how far the unequal basis of social relations is the result of agreement, have a powerful ideological message. Behind the stories of conflict and of divine appointment may lie a scenario in which a settled people engaged in agriculture was subjugated by newcomers (younger brothers, as it were) who imposed their own culture and belief system, inherent in the alien language they used through superior military skill and technology. The detail in the Scythian myth, where the golden objects catch fire, may be a direct allusion to the destructive methods used by aggressive nomads to subdue a vulnerable community of farmers.

There is plenty of archaeological evidence to support such an interpretation. The work of the Soviet scholar Marija Gimbutas on the Kurgan culture of the European steppe, has shown how the late Neolithic period in south-east Europe involved a gradual process of cultural shift. An essentially settled agricultural community, strongly matrilineal and evidently peaceful in character was overrun by a highly mobile and aggressive group of pastoralists. A comparison of the cultic objects of these very different societies shows a replacement of thousands of clay models of fertility goddesses by the warlike insignia of a religion devoted to sun- and sky-worship of a kind that echoes Herodotus's account of the Scythian myth. Changes of burial practice also emphasize the shift towards a much more patriarchal organization of society. Maryana Khlobystina, who has investigated burial practices along the banks of the river Volga, reports that the vast majority of burials were reserved for males and children, thus demonstrating the drastic relegation of women within Steppe society during the late Neolithic period.

The proto-lexicon of the Indo-Europeans supplies numerous hints of an ideological formation weighted towards hierarchical, patriarchal, aggressive elements, and the findings of Russian and Eastern European archaeologists have confirmed this bias. It seems remarkable that languages stemming from a proto-Indo-European original have spread into nearly every continent, where their use, for the most part, has coincided with the propagation of aggressively hierarchical and patriarchal social structures. The connection between the many factors at work is palpable, though it is also variable; one would like to be able to decide what role was played in the development of palaeolinguistics itself by the medieval tradition which held that the three sons of Noah – Shem, Japhet and Ham – were representatives of the three estates, of priests, warriors and cultivators. In the prehistory of language, there have been numerous episodes in which religion or ideology was instrumental in the distribution of a particular language. What needs to be stressed is the reverse possibility of languages having a decisive function in the development and interaction of social systems and ideological frameworks.

I have already suggested how difficult it is to avoid this conclusion when observing the distribution of languages during the historic – as opposed to prehistoric – period. Sometimes a complete interdependence of language and ideology focuses on the authority vested in a particular book or books. Clearly, the cultural significance of one book, the Koran, has been the motive force behind the spread of both the Arabic language and the religion of Islam. Although Islam claims to be a world religion, its adherents are dubious about the possibility of its message being transmitted adequately by means of any language other than Arabic. One recent commentator gives expression to this linguistic chauvinism in a particularly graphic manner:

> Some communities have severed their ties with the Arabic tongue – the language of the Qur'an – and started writing in Latin after generations of Arabic calligraphy. Antagonism, strife and even open war have repeatedly flared up between erstwhile brethren in one or the other part of the Muslim world.[7]

At the same time, the exceptionally stable condition of Arabic, which has undergone remarkably little change in the last 1500 years, is attributed to the influence of the Koran itself. Unlike most religions, Islam is founded on the conviction that its sacred text is literally the word of God; maintaining the purity of the language in which it is composed amounts to a sacred trust. The centrality of writing to Islamic culture is conveyed by its classification of mankind into three categories: Muslims, the other monotheists, and the rest. The other monotheists, the Jews and Christians, are referred to as the 'people of the Book'. Paradoxically, the Koran was the *only* book in the Islamic world for several generations. Even more paradoxically, its text was established, and fiercely preserved, in an exclusively oral, and illiterate, culture. Until shortly after Mohammed's death, it existed solely in the memories of the 'Koran bearers', followers of the Prophet who had learned the sacred words by heart. It was not until the battle of Al-Yamamah, in which 70 of these oral witnesses were killed, that it became expedient to insure against the possible loss of the oral account by actually putting down the text in writing. Most extraordinary of all is the status accorded to writing in a text composed orally which nevertheless refers self-reflexively to the words 'pen' and 'book' on several occasions.

The anchor which language finds in religion, and vice versa, has had an incalculable impact in cultural history. The decisive importance of sacred texts acting upon the patterns of language distribution and ideological influence is perhaps clearest of all in the early history of the Christian church. Recent work on the Dead Sea Scrolls raises questions about the status of early Christian texts and in particular about the writings of St Paul.[8] Many of the Scrolls, although they share

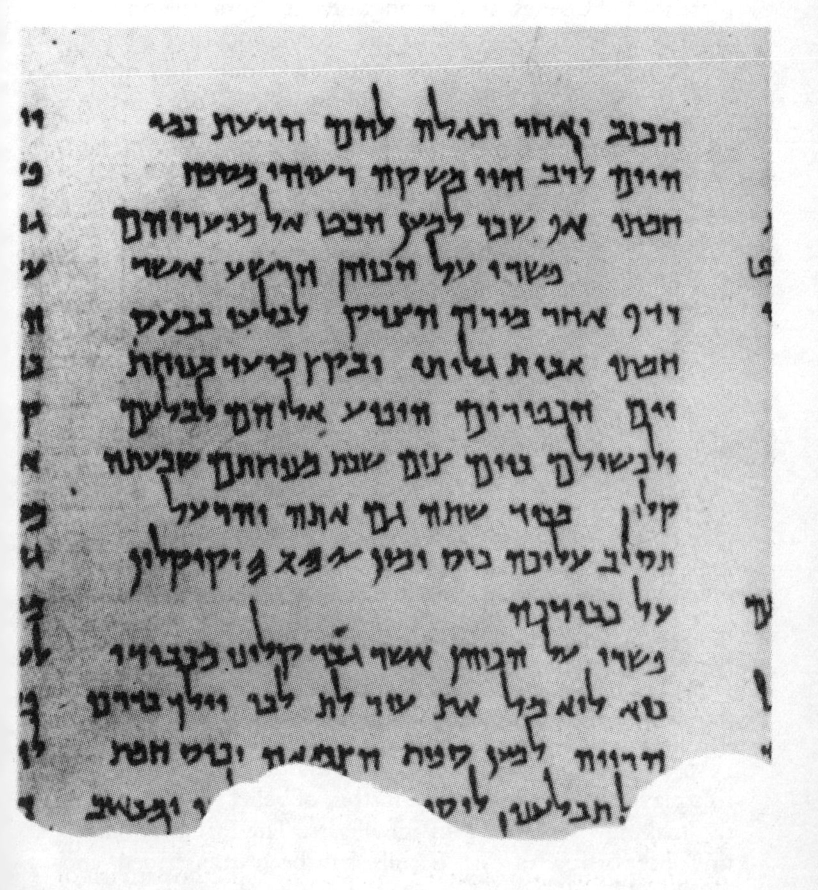

A fragment of the Habakkuk Commentary, one of the Dead Sea Scrolls.

a great number of linguistic formulae with the gospels, present a radically different interpretation of the Christian message from that of the Pauline inheritance. Fiercely traditional, unswerving in their adherence to 'the law', they not only present Christ as an orthodox Essene, they also appear to present the Essenes as indistinguishable from the militant Zealots, violently opposed to any accommodation with the secular power of Rome and completely out of sympathy with Paul's mission to convert other peoples to the Christian faith. Indeed, it may be that Paul himself is the figure referred to as 'the liar' in a crucial text that is now known as the 'Habakkuk Commentary'; in this, a figure who resembles Paul is pitted against a 'Teacher of Righteousness', who may have been St James, the brother of Jesus. The Essene version of the Christian message is jealously nationalist, deeply embroiled in the politics of civil disobedience. It offers a perspective on the events of the first century AD which casts it as ideologically narrow but also as more broadly based and commanding more popular support than the version we have received of the history of the early Church would lead us to suspect. One reason why it has been completely eclipsed by the legacy of St Paul may have to do with the language, or languages, in which it is enshrined. Paul's international mission was propounded in Greek, one of the two international languages of the day: the Essenes' self-protective and inward-turning creed was secreted in the local, and dying, languages of Hebrew and Aramaic.

Moreover, the re-emergence of these extraordinary texts by the retrieval of the Dead Sea Scrolls between 1947 and 1956 has provoked a further demonstration of the formidable role played by language in the history of belief systems, and in the making or breaking of ideologies. The fact that only a tiny proportion of the Scrolls has been transcribed and published in the 45 years since that first discovery cannot be entirely divorced from the nature of the threat they pose to the basis of the Church. A majority of the most important texts has been monopolized by a team of Catholic scholars linked to the Congregation for the Doctrine of Faith, the Vatican body that used to be known as the Holy Inquisition.

It is only recently that independent scholars have been able to acquire sufficient evidence, by extraordinary means, to propose that these fragments of papyrus offer an entirely new context for the wording of certain key phrases in the gospels that would utterly revolutionize their meaning. For this reason, it is in the interests of certain elements in the Church that the language of the Scrolls should as far as possible be suppressed. The connection between language distribution and the spread of religions needs to be enlarged to confront the realities of power relations and the evolution of political structures and social systems.

CHAPTER FOUR

ON PAROLE: LANGUAGE IN SOCIETY

CHAPTER FOUR

ON PAROLE: LANGUAGE IN SOCIETY

> Everyone should have two voices, the one truthful, the other natural.
>
> Euripides

Greek was the language in which and for which the first proper alphabet was developed, but it is now better known for its link with another beginning: the first stirrings of modern political democracy. In its way, this second great beginning was no less important in the history of language-use than the devising of an alphabetical system. The fledgling democracy required new and more extensive uses of language in order to regulate itself; the sudden and dramatically increased participation of large numbers of people in the political process foregrounded the need for rhetorical skills. Additionally, the written record came to embody the will of the state, since this could no longer be identified with any individual. Under the individual tyrant, the conduct of government relied on the issuing of orders that must be obeyed without discussion. Under democracy, every decision was the outcome of protracted debate and negotiation, stimulating the development of tactics of persuasion and deterrence. All at once, the ability to manipulate language was of supreme importance.

As soon as this new political culture had arisen, it precipitated a crisis of faith in the ability of words to mean what they say. If political power now lay within reach of those who had neither inherited it nor taken it through force of arms, but who had begun to acquire it by means of their control over language, clearly the motivation behind the desire to become an effective public speaker could be less than totally disinterested. Not everyone in the citizens' Assembly taking part in a debate would be animated by a love of the truth. Those who sought to persuade others to adopt their own point of view might be working in their own interests as much as, if not more than, in the interests of the majority: the language they used might be designed to camouflage, rather than reveal, the truth. The strength of the new democratic system immediately threatened to turn into its greatest weakness: a weakness that could easily have been exploited by those now being educated for the first time in the methods of a new school of philosophers – the Sophists.

The Sophists, notorious for being able, in Socrates' phrase, to 'make the worse argument appear the better', were perhaps most dangerous because they offered a serious philosophical validation of the idea that language 'can appeal to truth, profess truth, but not attain it.'[1] But in practical terms, their influence was greater in the form of the tuition they offered to ambitious young men from well-to-do Athenian households, youths whose eagerness to make their presence felt in political life was much less informed by an awareness of traditional values than would be the case for an older, 'non-democratic' generation. The moral vulnerability of Athenian youth was badly exposed by the growing demand for the kind of rhetorical expertise that the Sophists could teach, and further assailed by the fact that the Sophists took money for their services. They were also, for the most part, non-Athenians: inhabitants of the city whose sense of allegiance to the Athenian state must have been questionable if not wholly inoperative. If the motives of both pupils and teachers were compromised, and the pedagogic process they were engaged in ultimately undermined the relationship of language to truth, then the disadvantages of the new democratic culture had a significance perhaps more far-reaching than its obvious advantages. On the other hand, some of the more demoralizing – and amusing – side-effects might be reserved for the Sophists themselves, as Socrates is supposed to have shrewdly observed:

> The case of the professed statesman is, I believe, very much like that of the professed sophist; for the sophists, although they are wise men, are nevertheless guilty of a strange piece of folly; professing to be teachers of virtue, they will often accuse their disciples of wronging them, and defrauding them of their pay, and showing no gratitude for their services. Yet what can be more absurd than that men who have become just and good, and whose injustice has been taken away from them, and who have had justice implanted in them by their teachers, should act unjustly by reason of the injustice which is not in them? Can anything be more irrational, my friend, than this?[2]

But regardless of the extent to which the moral relativism allowed by the workings of democracy may or may not have backfired in respect of individual sophists, or statesmen, the central reality of Greek culture at the beginning of the fifth century BC was that language was being given a greater social and political scope than it had ever previously had, while its reliability as a medium for conveying truth, meaning and value was being subjected to a greater number of theoretical and practical assaults, at exactly the same time.

It is difficult to underestimate the sense of dislocation and readjustment that must have accompanied the transition from a tyrannical to a democratic way of life. The destabilizing of the Greek language that occurred during this historical episode is not simply a form of reaction to changes in the executive functions of government; it is an intrinsic part of a wholesale revision of Greek culture and of a thoroughgoing redefinition of its basic values. During the archaic period, and under the rule of the *tyrannoi*, the fundamental social unit of the Athenian state was the household, or *oikos*. The state as a whole duplicated the structure of a set of hierarchical family relationships; the *tyrannos* was a magnified version of the patriarch at the head of each household. Social ties and loyalties were determined by blood relationships; the conditions of allegiance to the *tyrannos* were simply given, not agreed upon. With the move to a democratic system, the *oikos* retained a great deal of its importance, but onto the layer of social duties and responsibilities that it entailed there was now superimposed another layer of obligations. The fundamental social unit of the democratic state was the city itself, the *polis*; the citizen's sense of loyalty was now directed towards something more abstract than an individual ruler, and the feelings which bound him to others were less easy to grasp than the automatic affiliations conferred by an awareness of his place within a particular household and network of family relationships. The aggressive loyalties of the heroic age, which called quite precisely for devotion in every sense to individual heroes and their causes, were now obstructed by the rival claims of an impersonal entity; the citizen's sense of loyalty was diffracted and absorbed into a new collective enterprise. But not entirely, of course: *oikos* and *polis* existed, as social facts and conceptual frameworks, side by side. The division of the city into public and private spaces reflected the historical doubleness of fifth-century Athenian culture, which maintained contact with traditional attitudes while in the process of engendering a distinctly modern sensibility. What would an Athenian understand by the word 'loyalty' under such circumstances? The word would be subject to varying, not to say conflicting, pressures; it would carry a much greater complexity of meaning and would indicate a much greater epistemological tension than might have been the case a generation earlier. This extraordinary historical shift from one kind of society and culture to another was not only reflected in, it was also decided by, a struggle over language. The future of the new democratic state depended on its ability to give the underlying concepts of Greek culture a new set of references and to redefine the meaning of all its key value-words.

This contesting of the meanings of words crucial to the functioning of any society was nowhere more evident than in the literary form which now sprang into being and which has since become identified with classical Greek culture: tragedy. As Jean-Pierre Vernant has expressed it: 'The tragic message when understood, is precisely that there are zones of opacity and incommunicability in the words that men exchange.'[3] When opacity replaces transparency in the course of trying to understand what the organizing principles of society are or should be, the results are potentially devastating, not just for one or two protagonists but for the whole culture. This is the true scope of the tragic dilemma and it is rooted in what societies fail to agree upon in giving meanings to the languages they use. On the other hand, a complete lack of disagreement, a rigid consensus, produces ossification and sterile conformity; some degree of semantic revision and innovation is constantly needed for societies to be able to test their values and explore the limits of their assumptions. For the sake of cultural health, the tragic perspective must always be there.

All of these issues are explored and their implications pursued in the earliest surviving trilogy of the Greek tragic theatre, the *Oresteia* of Aeschylus. In thematic terms, the entire trilogy revolves around the ambiguity that had become attached to the concept of justice. The first play, the *Agamemnon*, deals with Agamemnon's return from the Trojan war to his palace at Argos, where he is killed by his wife Clytemnestra in retaliation for his own ritual sacrifice of their daughter Iphigeneia. In the second play, the *Choephoroi*, Orestes and Electra, the remaining children of Agamemnon and Clytemnestra, plot to avenge their father in an act of matricide that is eventually carried out by Orestes. In the third play, the *Eumenides*, Orestes, hounded by the Furies (the 'Erinyes') takes refuge at Athens, where the ethical dilemma provoked by his actions is resolved in a court of law, administered by Athenian citizens demonstrating the effective working of one of their new democratic institutions. But the jury is split down the middle and justice can only finally be done (which is to say, Orestes is vindicated) with the help of a casting vote from the goddess Athene, whose intervention both gives a divine sanction to the legal process and sets a limit on the ability of humankind to control its own affairs. Aeschylus effects a compromise between the ethos of the heroic age and that of a democratic era: between obedience to

Pompeian fresco, often referred to as a portrait of Sappho: a rare view from the ancient world of woman as writer (although the pen held across the lips suggests a prohibition of speech).

an absolute power that does not have to explain itself, and submission to a legal code that has a rational and consensual basis. In the course of the three plays, the Greek word for justice, *dike*, attracts to itself a multiplicity of meanings. Ultimately, it can refer either to the effect of a revenge-killing or to the outcome of a fair trial; the incompatibility of these two concepts of justice provides a graphic evocation of the semantic insecurity and cultural instability of Greek life during the period when the plays were first produced.

But although *dike* is probably the single most important word in the trilogy, it is only the most prominent example taken from a language that is prone to a constant slippage or fluctuation of meaning, in a series of dramatic situations that disclose the dangers of misunderstanding in a repeated struggle on the part of characters and audience to interpret signs, messages, portents and speeches that remain incorrigibly ambiguous. One of the most revealing aspects of this linguistic fallibility colours the ideological outlook of Greek tragedy as a whole, although it is already starkly evident in the *Oresteia*, and that is the link that is made between destructive and decadent kinds of ambiguity and the threat of transgressive behaviour with regard to the social role of women. The most powerful and skilfully manipulative orator in the trilogy is Clytemnestra, whose speeches are the more persuasive, and achieve a greater dramatic impact, almost to the extent that they deviate from the truth, or are calculatingly insincere. Clytemnestra is the average Athenian citizen's worst nightmare: she is a brilliant sophist who is also a woman.

Athenian democracy extended its rights and privileges only to native-born male householders; among those who were allowed to take part in the debates and cast their votes in the Assembly – and, less strictly, among those who attended the Dionysian festivals when the tragic dramas were performed – women, servants and foreigners were not included. If the control of political power was correlated with a control over language, then the right to define the meanings of words would be a jealously guarded privilege. The fixing of meanings could occur only in a way that reflected and reinforced the social superiority of men; the trial of Orestes reviews the death of Clytemnestra as 'justifiable homicide', while the murder of the patriarch is confirmed as much the more serious crime. Any form of challenge to the position from which male citizens speak is branded as irrational, even criminal or bestial – in the end, it becomes literally meaningless, since men determine what words mean. The most frequent sources of resistance to this formidable chauvinism and the conveyors of linguistic subversion are women, foreigners and (particularly in Euripides) that whole other dimension of the un-languaged, the instinctual forces of nature. The Greek word for foreigner, 'barbarian', is the onomatopoeic reflection of an outlandish, or incomprehensible, speech, which to Greek ears resembles the sounds that animals make: *bar-bar-bar*. Those who fail to make sense, the correct sense, in Greek inhabit a linguistic nullity and a social and political power vacuum.

To the Athenian male, the figure of woman remained irreducibly ambiguous. The citizen justified his privileged position by contrasting his own supposed rationalism with what was marked out as the passionate, even hysterical, nature of women, whose behaviour would be dictated less by the knowledge of an ethical code than by an inability to withstand sexual and other instinctual urges. Clytemnestra was one of the supreme examples, but she was only one amongst many; a whole series of women, of widely varying character, meet with destruction in Greek tragedy, in some degree through a standard disbelief in the sincerity of women's language. At the same time, a rejection of what was perceived as the irrationality of women had to co-exist with a means of incorporating women into the social structure of fifth-century Athens, where of course they were needed to maintain and reproduce the traditional social unit of the family. Within individual households, women functioned to a large extent in a biological role, although the symbolism of Athenian domestic culture actually enshrined the female principle in a way that totally obliterated this reality; at the centre of every household was the hearth, associated with Hestia, a tutelary deity whose symbolic representation of woman as virgin supplanted the biological condition of the real women who conceived and bore the children of Athenian families. The elevation of the female principle, then, entailed an ideological effacement of reproductive sexuality, the most important determining factor in the lives these fifth-century women actually led. And this sublimating manoeuvre, which appeared to raise the status of women at the same time as it defused the threat posed by their sexuality, was even more spectacularly evident in the representations of Athene, tutelary deity for the whole state. Athene, technically a woman, dressed and behaved like a general (she enters in the last play, hot-foot from settling a border disupute in Asia Minor). She became the very type of a controlled, a very masculine, aggression. In place of the hysterical and unpredictable violence of a Clytemnestra, she offered the shrewdly controlled violence of those who know how to stay in power. More than this, she was a woman whose own birth was supposed to have involved a complete circumvention of the female reproductive cycle. According to Hesiod and subsequent writers, she was born by springing fully armed and with a warlike shout from the forehead of her father Zeus: in every sense a creation of the male brain rather than of the female body. Also in the final play, the transmogrification of the wild, passionate, and extremely dangerous Erinyes ('furies') into the tamed, benign and emollient Eumenides ('kindly ones') offers another reflection of the same ideological process.

The Athenian male citizen inhabited a social space in which, both individually and collectively, he was acquiring an increasing degree of control over both his political fortunes and the linguistic universe in which he operated. But if the coherence of his language was threatened with disruption by the contradictions and irregularities of those against whom he defined himself, of those who represented everything that he himself was not, this threat could equally well come from above as from below. If the unregulated speech of women and barbarians only served to confirm the citizen's sense of his own superiority, the bafflement and hesitation he experienced on encountering the language of the Gods served rather as a salutary, and often a savage, reminder of the limitations and impoverishment of his own particular brand of coherence. The Greek tragedies are filled with oracles, portents, auguries and divine instructions that create bewilderment and misunderstanding among their human recipients. In the *Choephoroi*, even Orestes asks, 'May I put my trust in oracles like these or not?' It is almost true to say that the authenticity of a divine message is guaranteed to the extent that it is indecipherable. In the *Oresteia* as a whole, the most important Gods after Athene herself include Hermes and Apollo. Hermes is of course the messenger of the Gods and the conveyor of souls to the underworld, but he is also the patron of thieves and liars, the guardian of those whose communications are deceptive, of those who are cryptic or 'hermetic'. Apollo has many aspects, but the one stressed by Aeschylus is the one broached by the epithet *loxias*, 'that which has to do with the logos' – that which has to do with the word, with language. Apollo's decisive connection with language derives from his position as presiding deity at the oracle of Delphi, the most important oracle in Greece, consulted by all the major Greek city-states in times of military or political crisis.

Oracular language is what separates classical Greek culture from its successors in the European Renaissance and distinguishes it sharply from the Christian era. Unlike the Jews, Christians and Moslems ('people of the Book') for whom the word of God had a written form, the Greeks possessed no sacred text. Although centuries of commentary produced an enormous number of variant readings of the scriptures, the commentators were animated by the conviction that it was possible to establish a proper text and arrive at a correct reading. For the Greeks, the equivalent was a very specific kind of verbal message, a mysterious encoded utterance delivered by a priestess in a delirious state. Divine speech was always transmitted in the form of a riddle, and often appeared nonsensical. It required great ingenuity to interpret it; and although the vehicle of this speech was always female, the decipherers were always male. If the word of God was contained in a particularly elusive form of speech that had to be construed by mere humans, it was open to every kind of misconstruction. Tragedy often arose when the will of the gods was expressed in a manner that remained totally unclear to the tragic protagonist.

Specifically with regard to language, Greek culture was founded on ambiguities. The major social and intellectual changes of the fifth century BC introduced a new complexity into the Athenians' understanding of themselves and of the world they were trying to reshape, but in a way this situation only exacerbated, gave a new momentum and a fresh bearing to, the kinds of ambivalence that were seated at the very heart of the oldest traditions of Greek thought. A sense of the limits and untrustworthiness of language was constrained by particular circumstances; conflicts over the meanings of important Greek words were historically rooted in a particular time and a particular place. But at the same time, the procedures of debate, dialogue and of dramatic opposition that were developed to elaborate and explore these linguistic and cultural tensions produced a set of workable forms that could be taken up and filled with the concerns of other times and places, engaged in similar episodes of cultural transformation. This has clearly been the case with regard to tragedy, whose forms were reactivated and filled with urgent new concerns at the time of Shakespeare. And the tragic agenda of testing the limits of man's ability to understand and control his environment by a rational use of language has equally well become the trajectory of psychoanalysis. There is no Greek tragedy whose language has included a more complete demonstration of this coupling of historical anxieties with transhistorical implications than the most famous one of them all – *Oedipus Tyrannos*.

At the start of this play, Oedipus occupies the very highest position in his society: he is a *tyrannos*. He has achieved this distinction entirely by virtue of his linguistic expertise, having deciphered a fragment of oracular language, the riddle of the sphinx. The subject of the riddle is the ages of man: 'What goes on four legs in the morning, two legs in the afternoon, and three legs in the evening?' The correct answer is the single word 'man'. The sphinx's text underlines the vulnerability and frailty of humankind, as well as the brevity of the human span – childhood, maturity and old age are symbolized by the phases of the diurnal cycle. This emphasis on weakness and mortality is not without significance for the unfolding of Oedipus's subsequent career.

As far as his subjects, the citizens of Thebes, are concerned, Oedipus is superhuman, although the priest who leads a representative band of supplicants to him at the start of the play is careful to stress that he is not 'the equal of gods', even if he is 'the first of men'. As far as the gods are concerned, however, Oedipus's grasp of divine speech is minimal; more than that, his interpretation of the sphinx's language is a fluke, which belies how in certain ways he is not the first but the last of men, the lowest of the low. While the citizens regard him as clairvoyant, the gods recognize that in most respects he is already blind.

In order to lift the curse and dispel the plague that is afflicting the city of Thebes, Oedipus has to identify the murderer of Laius and bring him to justice. His method of doing this is to conduct an investigation which turns into a superb example of the inductive process and of man's reasoning powers. What is most striking about this detective work is the extent to which it draws on the languages of philosphical, legal and scientific research then going through a surge of development in the intellectual excitement of the mid-fifth century BC. Oedipus's pursuit of the truth behind his own condition shares in the spirit of inquiry that defined the intellectual culture of the audiences watching the first few performances of the play. The Athenians, in pushing back the boundaries of knowledge in virtually all spheres and enlarging the scope of their philosophical and scientific vocabularies, must have felt themselves on the verge of realizing the ultimate ambition: of being in possession of enough knowledge of the world to be fully in control of it. Surely, nothing that remained hidden could stay beyond the reach of human reason for very long; perhaps man could be self-sufficient in the universe, once and for all the 'measure of all things'. To a pious and conservative outlook this possibility was hubristic and blasphemous, since it proposed man's complete independence from the divine. *Oedipus Tyrannos* as a whole demonstrates both the consummate skills of human reasoning and the relative status of what it can achieve. The human sphere, which is amenable to description in the language of common sense, is marked off at the extremes and separated from at least two other major areas of knowledge and experience that it cannot describe: the impenetrable and ineffable wisdom of the gods and the inarticulable and unassimilable impulses of the natual world.

These limits and possibilities are registered throughout the play, but they are given an individual focus in the figure of Oedipus himself. As a *tyrannos*, he is unusual in that he has acceded to power neither through inheritance nor through seizing it by force but uniquely by the exercise of his linguistic talents. He is, in other words, precisely the kind of tyrant who might emerge from a linguistically orientated democratic system. It is no accident that the lifespan of tragedy as a literary form in classical Athens coincided with the absence of tyrants from the political scene. One of tragedy's most important purposes was to rehearse the reasons for barring the return of the tyrannical form of government. The Athenians had devised an institutional means of siphoning off the overambitious elements in their community: ostracism. The practice of ostracism involved a meeting of the Assembly in which each citizen would write down the name of anyone whose personal prestige and influence had grown too great not to pose a threat to the continuance of the democratic system. There was no debate, nor any form of canvassing involved; the person whose name appeared on the greatest number of potsherds was simply expelled from the city. It was a very summary form of justice passed by the rest of the community on one of its members, and it was designed to identify potential tyrants, those who were capable of taking the law into their own hands, those who might want to dictate terms and give their own meanings to the words and concepts around which the social and political life of the city-state had organized itself.

Ostracism insisted on an upper limit of acceptable behaviour beyond which no responsible citizen would pass. There was an equivalent institution for promoting the awareness of a lower limit, and that involved the ritual expulsion of the *pharmakos*. The *pharmakos* (the word means simultaneously 'poison' and 'cure') was a figure selected from the lowest levels of society as a scapegoat who would be driven out of the city in a symbolic purging of everything that was vilest in the life of the community. The point about Oedipus is that he embodies both of these figures, the *pharmakos* and the target of ostracism – the moral pollutant who is nothing short of bestial *and* the charismatic leader who seems semi-divine. The unravelling of the language of reason starts with the character of Oedipus himself, since he is a contradiction in terms. For much of the play, the progress of the investigation, the methods of intelligence-gathering and the evidence of intellectual enlargement are sustained in a language that demonstrates man's ability to grasp and articulate his position in the world and the nature of his relationship with it. But this sense of orientation occurs only within a space cleared by forcing and keeping apart higher and lower forms of the unspeakable; it is only in the space in between these two limits that man can determine what is acceptable behaviour for a rational being, can work out what it means to be a citizen. In the case of Oedipus, this space is what ceases to exist when the ratiocinative triumph of his detective work leads to the savage paradox that sees the superhuman and the subhuman in him collapse into one another. The intellectual range that had seemed to distinguish the human begins to seem like the thinnest of partitions separating it from these now unignorable and overpowering dimensions of experience in which human language has little or nothing to convey. And it is then that all the words that deliver a fundamental sense of orientation and relationship, the names that are given to members of a family, cease to mean anything at all when the fact of incest renders every reference totally uncertain in respect of mother, father, son, daughter, brother, sister. The very first words of the play are 'Ω τέκνα' ('Oh, children'), uttered by Oedipus in his address to the citizens of Thebes. It is a choice of words that stresses how the family relations of the *oikos* provide a model for the social relations of the entire state. By the end of the play, Oedipus does not even know how to use these words in addressing the members of his own immediate family. In the space of two lines, he appeals to the same persons as if they are members of different generations:

> Where are you, children?
> Come, feel your brother's hands.[4]

From being the acknowledged master of words and meanings, he has become the most inept linguist in the whole of Thebes. His experience has confused two different kinds of love, distinguished from each other by the two Greek words φιλια and έρος. One expresses the kind of attachment that features in normal kinship relationships, the other stands for sexual love. According to the scholar Simon Goldhill, Oedipus' blindness to the reality of his own condition is most economically represented as a form of word-blindness in the protagonist's inability to read his own name.[5] His *tour de force* in unriddling the sphinx's challenge is acutely ironized by the etymological implications of οι-διπους, which could be taken to mean 'alas, two-footed'; this gives an unmistakeably tragic inflection to the sphinx's description of man, precisely when he is supposed to be at the height of his powers.

The succession of generations in the history of a family provides the individual with the most direct and easily graspable means of projecting himself or herself into a network of social relationships that has both a spatial and a temporal dimension. Social position is derived from the model of family relationships while the succession of generations provides a blueprint for the ways in which a society's passage through time combines elements of continuity with a modicum of change. Tragedy, as a literary form and as a major event in the history of a culture and its language, is really one way of describing the disruption of continuity, the acceleration of the pace of change and the perversion of the normal basis of relationships. In Shakespearean tragedy too, the experience of a culture testing its values and redefining the associated key terms is hardly ever presented without obstructions being placed in the way of the succession of generations. In *Macbeth*, *King Lear*, *Hamlet* and *Coriolanus*, to cite only the most obvious examples, outright war is waged between parents and children. Ultimately, the decisive battles are waged over who has the right to determine the meanings of those words needed to guarantee the most basic categories of existence.

In *Macbeth*, the protagonist interrupts the succession of generations in a royal dynasty by murdering Duncan, a divinely appointed king, and preventing his sons Malcolm and Donalbain from assuming power. He acts like a *tyrannos* in placing himself above the law, subverting the established order and exploiting its language for his own purposes. His first public act after the murder is to make an elaborately deceptive speech, and the appalling invalidity of his language is juxtaposed grotesquely with the antics of the porter, whose degradingly comic behaviour and verbal 'equivocations' testify to an impending general loss of control over words and meanings that become hopelessly dislocated from each other. But what are the qualities of the established order that Macbeth has devalued? If his own career demonstrates a naked self-interest, his linguistic deviance alerts the audience to the motivations behind the speech-acts of other characters as well, and raises the question whether officially sanctioned descriptions of the world and its relations are no less manipulative after their own fashion. The ideology of the court that Duncan presides over is articulated in a language that conflates natural, social and cosmic orders. When he promotes Macbeth to a position of greater power and prestige within the hierarchy of thanes, Duncan employs a verbal formula that presents this calculating political manoeuvre as nothing but the inevitable stage in a natural process:

> Welcome hither:
> I have begun to plant thee, and will labour
> To make thee full of growing.[6]

His language is designed to protect the interests of those in power by converting what is historically contingent into the expression of a permanent and universal condition, although his construction of reality, like Macbeth's, is imposed on a world of phenomena whose rhythms and arrangements do not reflect the human agenda. More than this, the utterances of both Macbeth *and* Duncan occasionally echo the riddling and incantatory speech of the witches, whose entirely unnatural business it is to cast spells and create illusions.

In order to maintain his own peculiar legislation of meanings, Macbeth has to cut the lines of transmission that ensure the perpetuation of conventional truths from one generation to another. Once he has committed the murder, he expends much of his energy in the circumvention of posterity. The play is filled with predicates of breeding and rearing, and with images of children and young animals that Macbeth is dedicated to exterminating, both metaphorically and, occasionally, literally (as in the case of Lady Macduff's children). Paradoxically, his own nemesis comes in the form of Macduff, one 'not of woman born', whose birth by caesarian section exempts him from the usual reproductive cycle; this may suggest how the attempt to give the lie to heredity and be self-generated – an ideological project that is expressed in biological terms – is nothing but a form of auto-destruction. Macbeth's demented campaign against futurity maroons him in a present divested of meaning, a 'tomorrow and tomorrow and tomorrow' that is illustrated by the futile repetitions of Lady Macbeth's sleepwalking routines. His unilateral declaration of meaning is intended to engross an entire country, but ends up by locking him into a nihilistic solipsism. The repercussions for the society he has hijacked involve a traumatic revision of its basic conditions and relations, and this is nowhere more forcefully expressed than in the dramatic confrontation of different definitions of the word 'man'. The first emphatic definition is offered by Lady Macbeth when she pressurizes Macbeth into regicide with a challenge to his virility. For her, the word 'man' has to convey the qualities of a warrior, and it shades pretty rapidly into associations of a brutal kind of manliness. However, Lady Macbeth's interpretation is far from being idiosyncratic; it is all of a piece with the systematic euphemizing of a culture that can designate as 'valour' the crudest form of butchery – the Captain who gives a report of Macbeth's defeat of Cawdor, allows that the former is 'valour's minion' once he has totally dismembered his opponent:

> . . . he unseam'd him from the nave to th' chops,
> And fix'd his head upon our battlements.[7]

The macho definition of what being a man is about is quietly but firmly resisted in the exchange between Malcolm and Macduff. The latter receives the news of the massacre of his wife and children – a personal disaster which Malcolm promptly attempts to turn into a motive for revenge in order to further his own military projects. Macduff begins by noting the childlessness of Macbeth:

> *Macduff.* He has no children – All my pretty ones?
> Did you say all? – O Hell-kite! – All?
> What, all my pretty chickens, and their dam,
> At one fell swoop?
> *Malcolm.* Dispute it like a man.
> *Macduff.* I shall do so;
> But I must also feel it as a man.[8]

Macduff's use of the word 'man' calls to mind some of the modern connotations of the word 'humanity'; it suggests a capacity for sympathy with others, for compassion. Malcolm's attitude, revealed in his use of the word, is worryingly close to Lady Macbeth's idea of masculine ferocity. He has already gone through an elaborate pretence of being a completely immoral and self-centred Machiavellian in order to draw Macduff into proving his own integrity; his acting is intended to be a hoax, but it is a completely successful hoax that shows he has all the skills of a practised sophist. When he announces the restoration of order at the end of the play, he does so using the ideologically charged language of Duncan (he talks of 'planting' the traditions anew). He uses both the language of the court and the language of wilful individualism far too opportunistically, so that his rhetorical claims to be setting life in Scotland back on a natural footing seem facile and unconvincing.

Macbeth is a political play; it was first performed during the reign of James I, a descendant of Banquo who figures in the play as progenitor of a 'line of kings', presented to Macbeth as a seemingly endless series of children. One should not underestimate the social and psychological impact of the royal succession of 1603, involving a change of dynasty, in which the childless Elizabeth was succeeded by the homosexual James VI of Scotland. This was hardly a smooth transition; certainly it produced little stability in the politics of the court, now dominated by Scottish favourites speaking in an accent incomprehensible to most English ears. The language of power had a new and almost foreign character. But the play and its language reflect other, ultimately more profound tensions in the shift from one form of social organization to another. Just as Greek tragedy catches the mood and preoccupations of a culture exchanging a system based on the *oikos* for one based on the *polis*, so Shakespearean tragedy, according to Brecht, functions as a series of 'junction points . . . where the new in his period collided with the old'.[9] The terrifying isolation of Macbeth is the cost of his refusal to inhabit the position conferred on him by the established order of society. He does not obey the rules; in language terms, he disarranges the syntax, attempts to speak from a position he is normally barred from, strains to give a sense to words at odds with what is commonly understood by them. His is a world in which the language becomes freighted with private meanings, in which the predications of the self are allowed to overrule the predications of society, until he recognizes that the one-sided effort of adding new meanings to words is liable to result in a subtraction of meaning; towards the end of the play he submits to the realization that his pursuit of 'honour', conceived as applause for aggressive bravado, has brought him nothing but an empty 'mouth-honour', divorcing the word from the usual contexts in which it takes on meaning: 'love, obedience, troops of friends,/I must not look to have.'[10] Macbeth is one of the first great exemplary casualties of the modern culture of individualism; but in all of Shakespeare's major tragedies, the project of self-creation, or 'self-fashioning',[11] not only has strong symbolic implications for the importance of family histories, lines of descent, primogeniture and inheritance in the cultural history of the West, it also has a critical effect on the social and philosophical role of language.

When we recall the language of these tragedies, we often remember the soliloquies of the major characters, the words they utter when they speak their thoughts aloud. This in itself suggests how far psychological realities have displaced social realities; it gives a sense of the growing awareness of the complexity and scope of subjectivity at the same time as it anticipates the reaction against an overinvestment in self-absorption. The character of Hamlet is the most notorious example of this dilemma; disabled from acting by excessive cogitation, he is at the same time aware of how his own mental operations have more substance and credibility than the unthinkable actions of others that he has learned about from a ghost. Both 'internal' and 'external' realities have their phantasmal sides, which is why Hamlet is concerned to give his experience material expression in language that takes on a durable form – he becomes obsessed with the need to elaborate his thoughts and explain his actions in writing. The self-generating individual can only ever have his or her sense of reality confirmed by the generation of texts, in the production of language that can take on a life independent of the train of thoughts and feelings that first produced it, in the provision this makes for interaction. Hamlet's immediate reaction after the disappearance of his father's ghost is to *write* in the 'table' of his memory, and thereafter the play incorporates an entire oeuvre of Hamlet's literary endeavours: poems, letters, recitations and speeches for inclusion in other plays. In a very real sense, his most urgent ambition is to 'tell my story', to give his own version of reality in a form that he himself has devised. At the moment of his death, this is precisely the legacy he wishes to transmit to succeeding generations; Horatio is entrusted with the story-telling, a task whose responsibilities he recognizes in his undertaking to 'truly deliver' it, although as soon as he opens his mouth he will start to make it his own.

In *King Lear* this paranoid ambition is checked at the outset, when Lear's version of the story he has intended his daughters should live up to is repudiated in ways he had least expected.

His wilful self-fashioning involves a total rejection of maternity, both in the suppression of any reference to the mother of his children and in his resistance to the nervous affliction of *hysterica passio*: 'O! how this mother swells up toward my heart'.[12] Lear's persistence in telling a story that no-one else accepts results in the destruction of the younger generation but also in the instructive process of re-examining and re-defining the key terms that identify the principles governing the society he has been at the head of. The language of this play is extraordinarily volatile; there is a violent and ruinous series of confrontations over the words 'nature', 'need' and (to come full circle) 'justice'. The meanings of 'sight' and 'blindness' go through a complete reversal, as do 'folly' and 'wisdom'. *King Lear* offers the most systematic accounting of what is at stake when the individual sets out to become, in the words of Coriolanus, 'author of himself'; it demonstrates how the rejection of authority through the authorship of new forms of language has a momentous effect in the shaping of societies.

The picture emerging from all these plays is that 'tragedy' is the result when a culture is no longer able to stabilize the meanings of its words; changes in the social and political structure can only be confirmed, indeed can only ever be realized, by the accomplished fact of changes in the language itself.

CHAPTER FIVE

WORLDS OF WORDS: UNIVERSAL GRAMMARS, ENCYCLOPAEDIC DICTIONARIES

CHAPTER FIVE

WORLDS OF WORDS: UNIVERSAL GRAMMARS, ENCYCLOPAEDIC DICTIONARIES

> And now the last is reaching the first and the end the beginning.
> All things are returning to their Original, where all parables, dark sayings, all languages, and all hidden things, are known, unfolded, and interpreted.
>
> Abiezer Coppe (1649)

Tragedy provides graphic examples of how language operates within a given society or culture, but the question of how languages function among and across societies and cultures is addressed with particular urgency and comprehensiveness in a whole series of seventeenth- and eighteenth-century intellectual projects. The encounter with foreign tongues, from at least the time of the Greeks, has often entailed a dismissal of 'barbarian' cultures and too often the barrier of mutual incomprehensibility has been thrown down from one side in the process of imperial expansion, whether military or economic. The first crime committed by Spaniards in the New World was the kidnapping of natives who could be turned into interpreters. In 1492, the same year in which Columbus forced his own language onto those he had enslaved, there was published the first grammar of any modern European language, Antonio de Nebrija's *Gramatica*. De Nebrija made the claim that language had always been the partner of empire, and when a copy of his book was presented to Queen Isabella by the Bishop of Avila, the Bishop's response to the Queen's rather bald inquiry, 'What is it for?' was to point out, 'Your Majesty, language is the perfect instrument of empire.'[1]

The development of grammar as an object of study has had a decisive effect on attitudes towards national, racial, social and regional identities, since the prescribing of what counts as 'good' grammar and the proscribing of what is regarded as 'bad' has often catered to prejudice and establishment values. From the start, the grammatical analysis of language has focused on written rather than spoken forms. Unsurprisingly, the western tradition began in the first century BC in Alexandria, which housed the greatest library of the ancient world, a vast storehouse of written texts that included, for example, copies of 78 of the 92 plays of Euripides (only 19 have survived the intervening centuries of destruction and neglect).

The earliest surviving authoritative work on grammar is the Greek *Art of Letters* by Dionysius Thrax. Of almost exactly the same antiquity (dating back to 100 BC) is the huge *De Lingua Latina* (*On the Latin Language*) by Varro; no more than five of its 25 volumes are still extant. Varro, like Thrax, was concerned with literary language above all else, but he was also prepared to attempt a comparative study of both Greek and Latin examples. Texts on grammar continued to focus on Latin for another 1500 years, until the expansion of print technology and the alignment of national self-consciousness with a more committed use of the vernacular encouraged scholars to work on their own native languages. But irrespective of the languages involved, a common emphasis of most grammarians has been on 'best' usage. An evaluative approach to the structural description of language has always been in place; and it has recently been reaffirmed, particularly in the United States and the United Kingdom where instruction in the rules of grammar has been made an integral part of the education policies of conservative administrations.

De Nebrija's *Gramatica* marked the beginning of a period in which national self-confidence coincided with colonial expansion. It was partly as a result of the discovery of new worlds leading to the realization that the number of languages in existence was far greater than had been suspected, and partly because the use of Latin as an international language was threatened by the use of vernacular languages with their constantly evolving structures, that serious attempts began to be made to forge a universal language. The colonial enterprise became an important extension of English culture in the sixteenth century, and it was from early in the following century that England started to become known as a centre for inventors of universal languages. At first, efforts were concentrated on the search for a universal alphabet, a system of characters into which all known languages could be transposed. Initial suggestions by Francis Bacon were worked up into fully detailed schemes by Francis Lodwick in *A Common Writing* (1647) and Cave Beck in *The Universal Character* (1657). But the devising of a 'language-converter', although it might seem to hold out the prospect of a practical application, did not go far enough to satisfy the philosophical ambitions of those for whom the imperfections of natural languages might be redeemed in the structure of an artificial, universal one; for this ought to offer a perfect reflection of the rational order of the world. In Britain, Lodwick, Samuel Hartlib, George Dalgarno and John Wilkins were all working along these lines. In general, the British school of inventors held to the empiricist approach that language reflected an order of objects in the sensible world, an approach that became instituted in the strictures of the Royal Society under Thomas Sprat. Sprat recommended that all language should approximate to a 'naked, natural way of speaking' that would not permit interference with the mechanical transfer of meaning. Virtually every theory produced in this context included some version of the proposition that 'words are the signs of things', although many surrounded this truism with a manner of presentation that belied it.

Perhaps the most contradictory and revealing of all proposals for a Universal Language was that of Sir Thomas Urquhart, the first English translator of Rabelais. What is particularly interesting about Urquhart's scheme is the combination of its patently absurd claims and the transparency of its author's motives, which are political, religious and

Logopandecteiſion,

OR AN

INTRODVCTION

TO THE

VNIVERSAL LANGVAGE.

Digeſted into theſe Six ſeveral Books,

Neaudethaumata,		*Chryſeomyſtes,*
Chreſtaſebeia,		*Neleodicaſtes,* &
Cleronomaporia,		*Philoponauxeſis.*

BY

Sir THOMAS URQUHART of *Cromartie*, Knight.

Now lately contrived and publiſhed both for his own utilitie, and that of all pregnant and ingenious Spirits.

Cœdere quarenti nonne hac juſtiſſima res eſt?
Qui non plura cupit, quam ratio ipſa jubet.
Engliſhed thus,
To grant him his demands were it not juſt?
Who craves no more, then reaſon ſayes he muſt.

LONDON

Printed, and are to be ſold by *Giles Calvert* at the *Black-ſpread-Eagle* at the Weſt-end of *Pauls*; and by *Richard Tomlins* at the Sun and Bible near *Pye-corner*. 1653.

economic. Urquhart's *Logopandecteison, or an Introduction to the Universal Language* was published in 1653, during the English Civil War, but his first attempt to interest potential sponsors came in the form of an appeal to the Council of State just three weeks after the Battle of Worcester in 1651. Urquhart was a life long royalist whose loyalties were first declared when he took up arms against the Scottish Covenanters in 1638. Although he was the eldest son of the Laird of Cromarty, he inherited nothing but an insupportable burden of debts that supplied a *leitmotiv* for all his writings. The loss of his own patrimony coincided with the national interregnum and these two breaches in the law of succession had a profound effect on the direction of his work. The year before *Logopandecteison* appeared, he published the eccentric *Pantochronochanon: or, A peculiar promptuary of time*, which was nothing more nor less than a family tree. It purported to trace the line of the Urquharts back through the chieftains of ancient Greece as far as Adam himself. A critical stage was reached with the generation of the sons of Noah when, appropriately enough, the Urquhart strain was supposed to have passed through the ancestor of all the European languages, the redoubtable Japhet. Sir Thomas's paranoid relish for meaninglessly exhaustive detail has two particularly significant aspects: it asserts the ultimate value of continuity and tradition at a time when even the royal genealogy has been rendered worthless; and it correlates the decadence of family stocks with the corruption of languages as they diverge from the 'most ancient and honourable stem':

> How, by the iniquity of time, and confusion of languages, their names have been varied, their coat Armour altered, and as new scions transplanted unto another soil, without any reference almost to the stock from whence they sprung.[2]

As a kind of preface to the theory of the universal language, the *Pantochronochanon* begins to identify the political motive behind Urquhart's attempt to promote the restoration of order in the linguistic universe. With the king beheaded and his power usurped, with Urquhart's own family name dishonoured and his inheritance dispersed, with his writings scattered and mostly destroyed in the aftermath of the Battle of Worcester, Urquhart writes from his prison cell a theory of language that does not stop short of renaming everything in the entire world:

> He confuteth that disproportion in matter of number twixt words and things, wherewith the smatterers in knowledge would cloak their inability of giving unto everything its proper term . . . .[3]

Only by absolutely engrossing the entirety of phenomena with an equivalent form of words will Urquhart be able to re-organize a world that is controlled by his political enemies, given direction by his religious opponents, and ransacked by his creditors.

He begins his work with a dedication to 'Nobody' – the only figure who was generous and helpful to him after the defeat at Worcester. The gesture is a typically playful one, but it is also the very clear expression of a desire not to be in anyone's debt. Urquhart's desire that his language should occupy all the available linguistic space, that his names for things should exist in a proprietorial relationship with them, is also expressed in the frequent analogy he employs between the elements of a language and the elements of a building, or complex of buildings. Although he writes from confinement, 'cooped up within walls', his imagination allows him to compare the mastery of his language with the ownership of 'storehouses', the occupancy of 'houses', and the super-intendence of entire cities:

> This world of words hath but two hundred and fifty prime radices, upon which all the rest are branched: for better understanding whereof, with all its dependent boughs, sprigs and ramelets, I have before my lexicon set down the division thereof (making use of another allegory) into so many cities, which are subdivided into streets, then again into lanes, those into houses, these into stories, whereof each room standeth for a word; and all these so methodically, that who observeth my precepts therein shall at the first hearing of a word know to what city it

> belongeth, and consequently not to be ignorant of some general signification thereof, till after a most exact prying into all its letters, finding the street, lane, house, story and room thereby denoted, he punctually hit upon the very proper thing it represents in its most specifical signification.[4]

The abrupt exchange of 'allegories', whereby the structure of the language is compared first with naturally evolving forms and then with the civic, social reality of an artificial order imposed by men is extremely revealing of Urquhart's underlying intentions. Although he is constantly asserting that he 'plainly setteth down the analogy that ought to be betwixt things and words', the real use of his language is to be a medium of communication for a whole set of social, political and economic relations that will rival the existing state of affairs. The strong biases of Urquhart's writings are nowhere more apparent than in the sheer unlikelihood of most of his claims. Since the perfect order that his language reflects includes many more categories of being and parts of speech than have ever been previously disclosed, the rather blatant implication is that the social 'levelling' of the English Revolution has tended towards a homogeneity that ignores the intricate stratifications of what Urquhart regards as an authentic order of reality. For him, there are no fewer than eleven cases, eleven genders and four numbers ('singular, dual, plural, and redual'), while in respect of predicates, there are four voices and seven moods. The exaggerated nature of many of the claims is made possible by their non-specific nature; the sheer volume of impossibilities gives the work every appearance of being a parody of its chosen genre:

> So great energy to every meanest constitutive part of a word in this language is appropriated that one word thereof, though but of seven syllables at most shall comprehend that which no language else in the world is able to express in fewer than fourscore and fifteen several words . . .
>
> For variety of diction in each part of speech, it surmounteth all the languages in the world . . .

> Every word in this language, declinable or indeclinable, hath at least ten several synonyms . . .
>
> Every word in this language signifieth as well backward as forward . . .
>
> This language affordeth so concise words for numbering, that the number for setting down whereof would require in vulgar arithmetic more figures in a row than there might be grains of sand containable from the centre of the earth to the highest heavens, is in it expressed by two letters . . .
>
> The greatest wonder of all is that of all the languages of the world it is easiest to learn; a boy of ten years old being able to attain to the knowledge thereof in three month's space . . . .[5]

Urquhart's persistent overreaching is the expression of a desire for plenitude which stems from the experience of scarcity. With the loss of his political, religious and economic inheritance, he tries to create something out of nothing, to legislate meaning in the most total manner possible. In its sheer prodigality, his positing of unthought-of conditions and relations of being is part of an almost hysterical effort to outstrip the prevailing modes of definition; the production of an uncontainable excess marks the limits of the official languages of Puritan England. It comes as no surprise that Urquhart's next project should have been a translation of the works of Rabelais; and perhaps it is no more surprising that he managed to expand the printed bulk of *Gargantua and Pantagruel* to a third as much again through his inability to stop himself coining neologisms and multiplying connotations. Clearly, the unbridled creativity of his own style was at odds with the principal aim of his linguistic scheme, which was to police the uncertain boundaries between words, minds and things and establish the unshakeable rules of a universal grammar. In the case of his own writing, the policing operation was constantly subverted from within, although the need for order and the inclination to misrule were equally strong. Urquhart's central impulse seems to have been to advertise the degree of his own individual originality in relation to the strictly traditional values of a royalist, Anglican and aristocratic, land-owning outlook. The collective originality of a culture that had abolished at one stroke the importance of pedigree and that had questioned every form of authority, by the establishment of a commonwealth and the normalization of dissent, was resisted in his writing at every level. The second book of his language scheme is almost entirely devoted to challenging his creditors, whose depredations of his own wealth have retarded his ability to 'display before the world ware of greater value than ever from the East Indias were brought in ships to Europe'. In the 'Design of the Third Book', he again correlates the history of language families with that of human families, and stresses the need for unbroken lines of transmission, 'out of his respect to antiquity, his piety to succession'. In the end, he is most successful in arguing the universal basis, not of his linguistic fantasies, but of a cultural conservatism of the sort that has animated his own endeavours; 'he deduceth from the laws and customs of all nations, the tender care that ought to be had in the preservation of ancient families'. The beheading of the king has destroyed the very foundation of this tradition, and has assisted the process whereby the allocation of privilege on the basis of nobility gives way increasingly to the allocation of privilege on the basis of financial solvency. For Urquhart, the value of his birthright is unquantifiable, just as the value of the theories he is forced to sell in order to be able to survive cannot be set at a market rate:

> this vendacity should never have appeared in me of a commodity which to appreciate at the rate of any coin I would have accounted a kind of simony, and a course which, had my land been as clear of merchants as my mind is of mercinariness I had not deigned to stoop to for a kingdom.[6]

For Urquhart and his Royalist colleagues, 'the kingdom' is exactly the price paid in exchange for the new commonwealth. The only unlimited resources Urquhart has at his disposal are linguistic resources, and he resists the demands of those for whom an inheritance can be measured in financial terms, with a language that does not function as a medium for the straightforward transfer of meanings:

> Who deciphering the implacability of flagitators, by showing how they throw in obstacles, retarding their own payment, thereby tacitly to hasten his destruction and hinting at the unnatural breach of some of his fiduciaries, he particulariseth, the candour of his own endeavours, and nixuriency to give all men contentment, the discourse wherof, in all its periods, very well deserveth the serious animadversion of the ingenious reader.[7]

Although sense can be made of this, Urquhart's language is extravagant and obscure – it simply does not operate with standard units of meaning. In spite of his declared purpose to 'plainly set down' the analogy between words and things, Urquhart's actual practice of indulging an interest in the relations between words and words betrays the motive behind his language plan – it is cavalier in both senses. Its contradictions show perhaps more evidently than any similar project how an intellectual movement whose research is given such an abstract and universalizing character, is in fact driven forward by a desire to change the material distributions of wealth and power. And in the attempt to restore what has been deposed and to reaffirm its legitimacy, language both provides a myth of origin and descent and becomes the means of naturalizing it.

Contemporary with the vogue for 'universal language' projects was a growing interest in the possibility of composing viable dictionaries. It did not take long for dictionaries to become the textual embodiments of a world dominated by a respect for accurate classifications, fixed definitions and a stable order. The origins of dictionaries lay in the second millennium BC, when clay tablets containing lists of words in Sumerian glossed into Akkadian were used to instruct the Akkadians in the act of writing. The words were organized thematically rather than alphabetically, a practice reflected in the English equivalent of 1440, the *Promptorium parvulorum sive clericorum* of Galfridus Grammaticus, which provided a selection of important Latin terms glossed into English. The first important word-list in English to follow the alphabetical sequence was Robert Cawdrey's *Table Alphabeticall* of 1604, although its range was restricted to fewer than 3000 words. Cawdrey's experiment was soon emulated in the work of several competitors, including Henry Cockeram, whose *English Dictionarie* of 1623 was the first to be called such. It was not until the middle of the seventeenth century that dictionaries in English progressed beyond explaining the meanings of particularly difficult, often technical words. But with the publication in 1658 of Edward Philips's *A New Worlde of English Words* came the first approximation to the modern dictionary's all-inclusiveness. Philips's work was revised and expounded by John Kersey, whose own *New English Dictionary* of 1702 assumed the ambition of providing definitions for every known word in the language.

By 1755, the year in which Samuel Johnson published the most famous and influential dictionary in the English-speaking world, previous examples of the genre were both numerous and various. In effect, Johnson's work straddled two genres which we now tend to regard as separate although related – the dictionary and the encyclopaedia. In the process of illustrating the meanings of words, the lexicographer would draw upon a body of knowledge that his own text would specify, give authority to, and encapsulate. The choice of illustrative quotations was an act of discrimination that could never be impartial; it would elevate the status of some writers and relegate others, and it would establish an hierarchy among those branches of knowledge that were interinvolved in the culture of eighteenth-century England.

The standard view of lexicographers – and it was a view shared by Johnson himself to some extent – was that they were mere literary journeymen whose drudgery performed a useful, if somewhat undignified, function. Those who stood in most need of dictionaries would be regarded as rather second-class individuals according to the standards of the day: women, foreigners, the uneducated. At the same time, though, the relative insignificance of those to whom the lexicographer's work might be addressed could not ultimately detract from the nature and scope of the erudition involved.

The compiling of a dictionary, then, entailed an exercising of authority on an unprecedented scale. The lexicographer would determine what should be included in, and what should be excluded from, a body of knowledge that the pragmatic user of his work would learn to regard as the foundation of a national language and culture. The body of knowledge would be subject to stratification, thus helping to inculcate a sense of rank and respect for privilege identified by degrees of breadth of command over language-use. The dictionary could become an instrument of social control, dispensed indirectly and fostering assumptions that need not be insisted on too forcibly.

In some ways, the implicit, almost intangible, yet far-reaching and profound nature of the dictionary-maker's power is best captured through an allusion to the ancient privilege of a priestly class. Ephraim Chambers, whose own *Cyclopaedia or Universal Dictionary* (1728) is sometimes thought of as the main forerunner of Johnson's enterprise, speculated that the first dictionaries were devised in an archaic sacral context:

> Probably this was in the early days of the Egyptian sages, when words were more complex and obscure than now; and mystic symbols and hieroglyphics obtained; so that an explication of their marks or words might amount to a revelation of their whole inner philosophy: in which case, instead of a grammarian, we must put perhaps a priest or mystagogue at the head of Dictionaries.[8]

This hypothesis recalls the mysterious significance attached to writing by the illiterate and offers one further example of the symbolic power invested in Egyptian hieroglyphics by the western intellectual tradition. It turns the lexicographer's guardianship of the cultural tradition into a sacred trust and thus sanctions the privileged position of those who control the flow of information to the uninitiated. In another way, its sacralization of knowledge suggests that piety is the ultimate purpose of learning, and this would harmonize with Johnson's own assessment of the relative values of religious and secular discourses. His choice of texts as resources for illustration compose a hierarchy among the branches of knowledge in which revealed religion is given an importance far greater than the achievements of human reason. The extraordinary number of citations from writers subscribing to the elevation of faith over reason is a clear sign of Johnson's desire to check the growth of rationalism among the theologians of his own day. If the dictionary were to stand as an accurate reflection of the intellectual currents of the late seventeenth and early eighteenth centuries, it would incorporate many more references than it does to the work of deistic thinkers, yet Johnson more or less placed a moratorium on these.

Perhaps the neatest and most compelling indication of the religious partiality of Johnson's dictionary can be derived from one of its definitions:

> CRO'SSROW. *n.f.* [*cross* and *row*.] Alphabet; so named because a cross is placed at the beginning, to shew that the end of learning is piety.

The simple one-word definition triggers off what is clearly a personal reflection, indicating how the Dictionary is governed by certain ideological priorities at the most basic level of organization. The transparency of Johnson's interests is made particularly evident by contrast with the moderation of Chamber's *Cyclopaedia*, from which the word 'crossrow' is excluded.

That Johnson's ulterior purpose in compiling the Dictionary is to make it a channel for moral instruction, as well as a means of inducing its readers to recognize the authority of the Christian religion, is suggested by the frequency of allusions to homiletic works stressing the sinfulness of deceptive language. The primal sin is lying, which means that linguistic purity is a moral duty of inestimable significance. The following citation, from one of South's *Twelve Sermons* of 1692, indicates what is at stake when clarity of speech is unsuccessful or threatened: 'Christ saves the world, by undeceiving it.' The lexicographer's task, of 'undeceiving' the semi-literate, becomes a fundamentally Christian mission to restore the means by which the reader can achieve a state of grace. Johnson does not go so far as to assume that natural languages, once evolved, can be returned to an ideal, Edenic state, but his attitude towards definition does show something of an attempt to approximate to the primal act of naming, whereby any particular thing or idea can be given a single, distinct name. Any qualification of this distinctness leads to verbal and moral confusion. In Johnson's terms, the Dictionary resumes the full power of its imagined origin in a primal act of naming that is divinely sanctioned, and the genre to which it belongs becomes the most crucial and logical means of ensuring the constancy and stability of those verbal meanings that the best cultural traditions have accustomed us to. Dictionary-making is a more or less conservative undertaking: in Johnson's case, it supplies a pretext for reinforcing the political status quo, religious orthodoxy and cultural authoritarianism. Its technical criteria are designed to exclude insubordination, dissent, subversion – everything that offers to destabilize verbal meanings and social values by making them subject to what Johnson refers to as 'contestation':

> A definition is the only way whereby the meaning of words can be known, without leaving room for *contest* about it.

The ultimate effect of linguistic contest is the simultaneous disruption of moral, social and political realms. Johnson's sole illustration of the word 'crossrow' is a quotation from Shakespeare's *Richard III* which establishes a link between the basic organizing principle of the Dictionary and the security of the head of state:

> He hearkens after prophecies and dreams,
> And from the crossrow plucks the letter G;
> And says a wizard told him, that by G
> His issue disinherited should be.

This speech refers to the fears of Edward IV that his sons – destined to become the 'two little princes in the Tower' – will be murdered by a traitor whose name begins with 'G'. Johnson's illustration is particularly apt in that the protagonist of the play, Richard of Gloucester, is able to rely on the ambiguity which allows his own brother, George, Duke of Clarence, to be suspected in his place. Once again, linguistic stability is being identified with genealogical security, with the continuing viability of family histories. Alphabetical order is aligned with traditional social and political structures whose future is directly threatened by semantic uncertainty.

It is exactly the same scale of operations that is evoked by the Dictionary's definition of 'amphibology'. Johnson regards amphibology as a potentially lethal form of indefiniteness. He actually goes outside of English to furnish an illustration that can most effectively convey his deep distrust of verbal ambiguity:

> Discourse of uncertain meaning. It is distinguished from *equivocation*, which means the double signification of a single word; as *noli regem occidere*, *timere bonum est*, is *amphibology*; *captare lepores*, meaning by *lepores*; either hares or jests, is *equivocation*.

Johnson makes uncertainty a matter of life or death. The amphibology carries two utterly contradictory meanings:

> *noli regem occidere*, *timere bonum est*
> 'don't be afraid to kill the king; killing the king is a good thing'
> 'don't kill the king; it is right and proper to be in awe of him'

100 or so years after Urquhart's polemicizing when the memory of Charles I's beheading is still fresh, Johnson uses lexicography to issue warnings and reminders about the cost of breaking with linguistic and cultural traditions; innovation leads to a form of sophistry – it makes the worse argument appear the better – and its lack of semantic clarity is equated directly with an intent to deceive. This is particularly true in the instance just given; but it is also generally the case in the *Dictionary* as a whole that Johnson's choice and use of his materials reflect a powerfully sustained resistance to change.

As a rule, he avoids contemporary usage, and even contemporary literary writing; he is particularly opposed to new words entering the language, especially when they consist of borrowings from the French.

In view of all this, it is hardly surprising that, nearly 100 years later, in Thackeray's *Vanity Fair* (1848), Becky Sharp's act of flinging a copy of Johnson's Dictionary out of the window of her coach, as it departs from Miss Pinkerton's Establishment in Chiswick Mall, is meant to be viewed as a thoroughly revolutionary act. Miss Pinkerton is an educationalist, so called, whose reputation (and fortune) is derived from a single visit paid by Johnson to her school. Her practice of rewarding graduating pupils such as Becky with a copy of Johnson's book seems particularly incongruous in this academy, since her own sister Jemima does not even understand the use of a dictionary (she refers to it as a 'dixonary'). In this school, Johnson has been reduced, not altogether inappropriately, to a status symbol that will be recognized in 'polite' society.

At the same time as Miss Pinkerton is linked with Johnson, Becky is repeatedly brought into association with Napoleon Buonaparte. The most frequent historical references in the book are those which either anticipate or recapitulate the confrontation of the neighbouring states of France and England, and a majority of these references keep on coming back to the antagonistic role that Becky plays in English society, with her partly French ancestry and her linguistic competence, competence of a sort that is increasingly hard to come by during the protracted Napoleonic wars: 'she spoke French with purity and a Parisian accent', says the narrator, 'It was in those days rather a rare accomplishment'. In the initial episode of the book, a little crisis is reached with the confrontation between Becky and Miss Pinkerton, resulting in a psychological victory for Becky, made possible by the fact of her simply being part French and able to speak the language: 'thank heaven for French', Becky exclaims, 'Vive la France! Vive l'Empereur! Vive Buonaparte!'

What Becky's trouncing of Miss Pinkerton mainly suggests is the supersession of one historical epoch by another – the

Age of Johnson being energetically succeeded by the Age of Buonaparte. The description of Becky's departure along with Amelia Sedley from Chiswick Mall is accomplished with a literary echo of Milton's *Paradise Lost*: 'the great gates were closed', we are told, and 'the world is before the two young Ladies', just as for Adam and Eve, 'the world was all before them', at the point of entry into history, the moment when history starts, when men and women first experience historical time. Becky's jettisoning of her copy of the Dictionary is termed a 'heroical' act, and the constant emphasis on her French reminds the reader of the example provided by a nation and a society that had presumed to start history anew, as if for the first time, beginning again with the year 'one'. The expulsion from Paradise and the French Revolution were literally epoch-making events, but in the world of *Vanity Fair* it is as if epochs are made and superseded with the passing of every day. Towards the end of the second chapter the narrator tells us that 'if Rebecca was not beginning the world, she was beginning it over again', and her departure from Miss Pinkerton's is soon seen to be only the first of many such re-beginnings.

Once the step of abolishing the established order and existing conventions of knowledge has been taken unilaterally, there is little to prevent whatever replaces these things from being abolished in its turn, which makes history open up into a vista of bewildering relativities, where collective values cease to have any real meaning, efficacy or permanence. In other words, History abandons its grand narrative or master plot and enters a realm of discursive conflict, of semantic exhaustion and moral attrition. If the Age of the Great Lexicographer is over, if the dictionary is suddenly rendered useless, its respect for fixed definitions, stable order, classification, made redundant, that is because the world of *Vanity Fair* is filled with people like Becky who are constantly saying what they do not mean. Becky's skill with language is a skill that enables her to exploit the resources of the Dictionary precisely in order to conceal the intentions behind what she says rather than to ensure that her thoughts are exactly matched by her words.

The extensive use of the language of military conflict in *Vanity Fair* arises not just in order to reflect the campaigns that a military novelist would find suitable for treatment but also, or even rather, because the would-be non-combatant novelist finds that he is dealing with a society marked by internal lines of conflict. It is not that the characters are constantly enacting pale imitations of the Battle of Waterloo (which provides the setting of one of the most famous chapters in the novel), it is rather that Waterloo represents merely an extension of the way a society operates that is constantly at war with itself. And besides, the struggle between the English and French is not the only theatre of war that provides a means of staging the domestic violence that renders inauthentic the lexicon of English social life. When the characters Dobbin and Cuff fight one another in the schoolyard in Chapter Five, it is in a combat that is given strong overtones of the Battle of Waterloo, but it is also likened to an event in America's War of Independence from England. Cuff is firmly cast as George III, reacting to the revolt of his North American colonies. Once again, it is a revolutionary society seeking an originary moment that is granted the victory. But Dobbin is not a romantic revolutionary leader even by virtue of historical allusion; he is the son of a grocer and heir to a business that earns him the nickname of 'Figs'. In the aristocratic climate of his school, he is almost universally held in contempt, despite the language of mercantilism that is constantly employed in respect of Wellington's troops; they are described as an army of good customers – 'creditable warriors' – nothing more nor less than the armed wing of Buonaparte's famous 'nation of shopkeepers'. Dobbin's virtues are wholly prosaic ones, his strengths the stolidly middle-class ones of self-sacrifice and perseverance. He prevails over the representatives of the English establishment, and is hopelessly unable to adapt to the requirements of an English education system that is designed for young aristocrats.

In this scenario, Thackeray provides another crucial insight into the politics of language-use in the early part of the nineteenth century. In particular, he explores the implications of language teaching in the British education system, and the relative status of the classical languages, English, and the other 'living tongues', especially French. The pattern for language teaching in Britain was effectively aligned with the distribution of power and privilege after the famous Leeds Grammar School case of 1805. The school wished to use its endowment to promote the teaching of the 'modern living languages', especially French, with a view to practical application in the mercantile context of the 'Town of Leeds [which] . . . had of late years increased very much in trade and population.'[9] But its application was turned down by the Lord Chancellor, whose judgement rested on the definition of grammar school to be found – and where else would one look for it? – in Johnson's Dictionary, no less. It was Johnson – who becomes such a seminal figure in *Vanity Fair* precisely because of his centrality in British culture as a whole – who ensured that the grammar schools continued to be schools for 'teaching grammatically the learned languages'. During the subsequent phase of British cultural development, English was displaced by Latin and Greek in prestigious schools, although it continued to be taught in dame schools, hedge schools and mechanics' institutes.

English was always taught by rote, never in a way that offered instruction in grammar. In *Vanity Fair*, Dobbin finds it impossible to learn Latin, and therefore impossible to acquire the rudiments of grammar. Grammar's scope is in its provision of a syntax of relationships; it gives the learner a place from which to speak and a set of rules to ensure the normative character of everything he or she might say. Grammar remains the heart and soul of an education system that Miss Pinkerton's academy can only pretend to emulate with the enshrining of Johnson's Dictionary. Dobbin abominates it, and in his unilateral withdrawal from the imperatives of a classical education, he is only aping the desires of his creator Thackeray, who openly detests the premium given to grammar in the British education system. Both Dobbin and Thackeray seek refuge from what they conceive of as the stifling regularities and the demands for regimentation that go with learning Greek and Latin, in a fantasy of the East, of an undisciplined orient whose art is asymmetrically imaginative (full of arabesques); they are drawn towards the magical rather than the rational, and steep themselves in an atmosphere of enchantment rather than be governed by the claims of logic.

Dobbin, then, repeats Thackeray's love-affair with the seductive East, plunging himself into a 'favourite copy of the *Arabian Nights*', and is 'away with Sinbad the Sailor in the Valley of Diamonds, or with Prince Ahmed and the Fairy Peribanou in that delightful cavern where the Prince found her, and whither we should all like to make a tour . . .'. But he is also a grocer. And his rejection of Latin grammar in some way reflects the situation of an English middle class denied the advantages of a classical education and forced to assert the values of self-education and self-help. Dobbin's victory in the set-to with Cuff does not represent the supremacy of a revolutionary romanticism (for which Napoleon would have been the prime vehicle) but the ascendancy of that other revolutionary group, the English bourgeoisie, and their breakthrough in achieving the establishment of *laissez-faire* trading practices. For all his interest in new beginnings, Thackeray does not pursue a radical revolutionary political agenda, he does not greet the prospect of major upheavals in the narrative of history, but seeks to promote the interests of reform in a multitude of small acts of reconstruction and revision. He attempts to renegotiate the terms of the social contract without fundamentally altering the main structures, or classifications, of society. The world of the 'Great Lexicographer' (Miss Pinkerton's description of Johnson) had rested on foundations whose stability had been lost. By the time *Vanity Fair* was published in 1848, revolutions were breaking out all over Europe and the Chartists were organizing the largest mass rally in British history in Hyde Park. The complicated episode of social and political instability that had led up to these events embroiled language in yet another series of engagements with the concepts of nationality, gender and class.

CHAPTER SIX

TIES OF THE TONGUE: LANGUAGE, NATION, CLASS AND GENDER

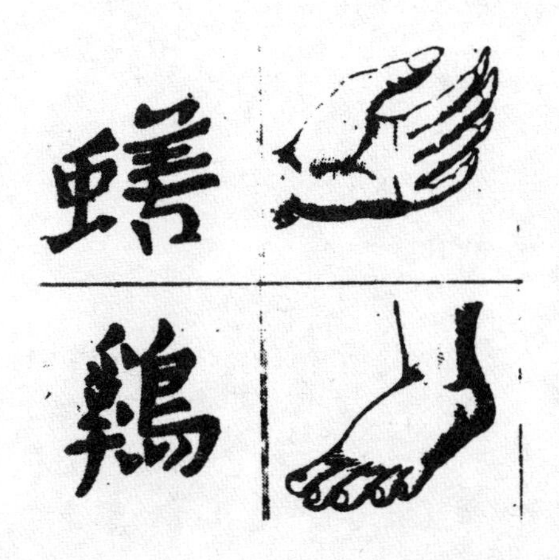

CHAPTER SIX

TIES OF THE TONGUE: LANGUAGE, NATION, CLASS AND GENDER

> Glamour girls are really grammar girls.
>
> Walter J. Ong

From the early 1790s to the late 1840s, from the time of the French and American Revolutions to that of the huge Chartist demonstrations in England, a language of conflict, disruption and renewal entered into and dominated the general awareness of how nations and societies were constructed and maintained. The extraordinary concentration of radical political thought and activity during this period presented a challenge not only to governments and administrations but also to those forms of cultural production that tried to sustain a belief in the need for stability, continuity, uniformity, subordination.

It was during this period in Britain that the study of the history of the language supplied a chief means of encouraging the British to think of themselves as a national unit, with a historical legacy that bound together, rather than split apart, the various peoples and social classes that inhabited the British Isles. This ambition of containment and regulation had historical roots that were reflected in linguistic habits dramatically different from American tendencies, which moved in an opposite direction towards a liberal inclusiveness, and allowed a much less troubled relationship between the individual speaker and the larger social unit.

Throughout Europe, philology became a discipline whose stress on precedent and tradition appeared to deny, while it really confirmed, the significance of the contemporary practice of re-naming, which involved not only the introduction of new concepts to old words (such as 'liberté, égalité, fraternité'), but also the use of new words to refer to old concepts (like the French Revolutionary calendar). The British philologists, who stressed the essentially British character of the history that lay embedded in words – 'language then is fossil poetry'[1] – were often closely identified with vested interests. Perhaps the best-known and most influential of these insiders was Archbishop Trench, whose eminent position within the Church helps to recall the ancient association between writing, sacred knowledge and sacerdotal privilege. Trench might be thought of as a particularly conspicuous example of the slightly conspiratorial figures responsible for the growth of philology described by Volosinov, the great Soviet linguist, in *Marxism and the Philosophy of Language*:

> The first philologists and linguists were always and everywhere *priests*. History knows no nation whose sacred writings or oral traditions were not to some degree in a language foreign and incomprehensible to the profane. To decipher the mystery of sacred words was the task meant to be carried out by priest–philologists.[2]

The point about the nineteenth-century priest–philologists that distinguishes them sharply from their ancient scribal forerunners, is that they had to cope with an increasing independence of thought in an era of widespread literacy. The priest needed to become a philologist, because the appeal to religious faith and doctrine was no longer enough to preserve traditional values and patterns of behaviour. The conservative project could now be more effectively served by paying attention to the social and cultural dimensions of language itself. If this had been the implicit programme behind Trench's writings, it was given an explicit rationale in the formulations of G.P. Marsh's *Lectures on the English Language*:

> It is evident therefore that unity of speech is essential to the unity of a people. Community of language is a stronger bond than identity of religion or government,

> and contemporaneous nations of one speech, however formally separated by differences of creed or of political organization, are essentially one in culture, one in tendency, one in influence.[3]

During the nineteenth century, language and nationhood were often virtually synonymous in the struggle of a number of small nations to break free of the imperial stranglehold of the great European powers. Clearly, this scenario did not apply in the case of English, which was itself the most rapidly expanding and influential of all the available languages of empire. However, the insistence on the Englishness of English makes sense in the context of the 'internal' colonizations of the British Isles carried out in one form or another from the very beginnings of the history of the language.

With the submission of the Welsh and the formal Acts of Union incorporating Scotland and Ireland into the United Kingdom in 1707 and 1801 respectively, the general use of spoken English became both the symbol and the means of eradicating the indigenous cultures of the Celtic peoples of Britain. The political necessity for instituting the 'language death' of Welsh and Gaelic is implied in Joseph Priestley's speculations on the alternative history of relations that might have developed between these difficult neighbours: 'the English and the Scotch, had the kingdoms continued separate, might have been distinct languages, having two different standards of writing'.[4] Matthew Arnold, although strongly attracted to certain characteristics that he identified with the Celtic temperament, gave lengthy, detailed and cogent expositions of the reasons for accelerating Celtic 'language death'. While he claimed to be charmed by the Celtic love of sentiment, beauty and spirituality, he was a great deal more suspicious of Celtic ineffectualness, absence of will-power, femininity – by the lack of qualities of firmness and resolve that he found unimpaired in the Teutonic races, particularly the Anglo-Saxon. Given this hierarchization of related Indo-European languages and peoples, it was inevitable that Arnold should canvass repeatedly for the consummation of a process that was already well advanced:

> . . . it must always be the desire of a Government to render its dominions, as far as possible, homogeneous, and to break down barriers to the freest intercourse between the different parts of them. Sooner or later, the difference of language between Wales and England will probably be effaced . . . and they are not the true friends of the Welsh people, who, from a romantic interest in their manners and traditions, would impede an event which is socially and politically so desirable for them.[5]

Arnold's was a distinctly nineteenth-century approach to the problem of cultural difference. His outlook was an unmistakeably imperial one, especially when compared with the liberal propositions of the eighteenth-century German philosopher Gottfried Herder, whose writings had done so much to establish the link between language and national identity. Herder had stressed the untranslatability of national cultures, the extent to which they may be contained *in*, and not simply expressed *by*, a given language. For Herder, each national culture had a unique value, which meant that the process of adaptation by, or assimilation into, another culture would result in the degradation of both. Between Herder and Arnold, in the first half of the nineteenth century, the work of Hegel, the Grimm brothers and Goethe made it possible to contemplate linguistic imperialism with a great deal more equanimity, since for them the principle of untranslatability was replaced by one of hierarchization; certain national languages and cultures were awarded a greater degree of relative importance than others.

Of course, the issues of translation were most fraught, and led to the greatest degree of resistance in the absorption of mainland British culture, for the Irish and their native Gaelic language. As late as 1843, the poet and polemicist Thomas Davis was marshalling the arguments of a latter-day Herder in defence of the untranslatable:

> the language which grows up with a people, is conformed to their organs, descriptive of their climate, constitution and manners, mingled inseparably with their history and their soil, fitted beyond any other language to express their prevalent thoughts in the most natural way. To impose

> another language on such a people is to send their history adrift among the accidents of translation . . .[6]

Davis's passion and eloquent stubbornness give some indication of why the British authorities poured so much money into the linguistic subjugation of the Irish throughout the first half of the nineteenth century. Between 1800 and 1849, the Government spent more on education in Ireland than it did on education in England, despite the fact that the population was less than one-eighth the size of England's. The teaching of English was standardized by granting the Kildare Place Society a virtual monopoly on the production of school text books. These books were typically deprived of any mode of instruction in grammar, and positively encouraged the use of a system of rote-learning of a kind that was later to become the butt of Dickens's satire. Rote-learning preempted individual initiative and turned language-acquisition into the prime method for inducing colonial subjects to obey rules without argument, and even without understanding. The British clearly thought so well of their arrangement for dealing with the turbulent Irish, that when the labour movement in England began to develop a significant momentum, it was thought expedient to adopt exactly the same procedures in British schools that had worked so efficiently in Ireland. In 1845 the government set up the National Society with the express aim of publishing and distributing in England the text books developed by the Kildare Place Society.

The politics of language with regard to nationality can be elided with contemporaneous debates about the significance of social class. The title of Benjamin Disraeli's 1848 novel, *Sybil: or, the Two Nations*, shows how the two halves of British society, separated by unequal divisions of wealth and property, could regard each other with the scepticism usually reserved for aliens. Once again, education became an arena of fundamental conflict; control over the language of teaching and learning was of critical importance for the authorities. Robert Lowe, Chancellor of the Exchequer during the period of the Second Reform Bill (1867), was distinctly anti-

Reformist in the sentiments he displayed in his contemporaneous essay *Primary and Classical Education*, published shortly before his assumption of high office:

> The lower classes ought to be educated to discharge the duties cast upon them. They should also be educated that they may appreciate and defer to a higher cultivation when they meet it, and the higher class ought to be educated in a very different manner, in order that they may exhibit to the lower classes that higher education to which, if it were shown to them, they would bow down and revere.[7]

Learning by rote enabled the 'lower' classes to recognize linguistic standards when they met them, although it also deprived them of the resourcefulness that would enable them to make their own utterances conform with the standards of speech employed by the 'higher' classes. By the end of the century the 'standard' language had become 'a class dialect more than a local dialect: it is the language of the educated all over Great Britain'.[8] The educated classes spoke English correctly, and in their possession of this capacity they were also guardians of the language, preservers of the cultural tradition, and masters of the national history. Official schooling aimed at obliterating class and regional dialects as part of the creation of a 'standard' language that was distinctly non-standard in origin. The result often took the form of an alienating split, as the educated norm was attended to in formal situations while the demotic was reserved for informal use as much as it ever had been:

> children learned two codes: first, the 'written language' and its spoken standard version . . . and second, the language of 'everyday talk'. The acquisition and practice of the 'standard language', however, evidently stopped at the school gates . . .[9]

While this suggests a certain resilience on the part of the non-standard, and even seems to point to the superior vitality of an authentic working-class culture, it is also of course the case that children who do not speak the 'standard' language outside the schoolyard are more than likely to exclude

Thackeray's sketch of Dr Johnson and Oliver Goldsmith: the solemn self-absorption of the 'great lexicographer' is contrasted with the playfulness – and disrespect – of the ragged, and therefore untutored, children.

themselves from the positions of power and privilege that go along with it. This point is very firmly grasped in Emily Brontë's novel *Wuthering Heights* which deals with the fortunes of two successive generations of lovers; in the earlier generation, the male protagonist Heathcliff maintains an antagonistic relationship with the culture of privilege, while the male protagonist in the later generation, Hareton, becomes absorbed into it. The process of assimilation could not be accomplished without education, specifically by Hareton's being taught how to read. Once he is able to decipher his own name in the inscription over the entrance to Wuthering Heights, he is nearly in a position where he is ready to inherit the property. His access to middle-class sensibility seems assured when his lover, Catherine, offers him lessons in genteel pronunciation in the closing stages of the book:

> 'Con-*trary*!' said a voice, as sweet as a silver bell – 'That for the third time, you dunce! I'm not going to tell you, again – Recollect, or I pull your hair!'
>
> 'Contrary, then,' answered another, in deep, but softened tones. 'And now, kiss me, for minding so well.'[10]

Paradoxically, the correct pronunciation of the word 'contrary' becomes the measure of Hareton's no longer *being* contrary, in social terms.

By 1847, the date of publication of *Wuthering Heights*, the 'standard' language had become almost completely identified with the accents of authority. This in itself indicates the degree to which the work of the philologists had successfully conflated questions of linguistic conformity with those of national security, but the equation had been examined in a quite different light, thirty years earlier in the work of William Cobbett. Cobbett's *A Grammar of the English Language* (1818) had offered instruction in correct usage, but his attitude towards correct usage was based on the supposition that attending to the rules of grammar did not in any way imply ultimate submission to the rules of the political establishment: far from it. His entire aim in publishing the book, he noted in the *Political Register* of 29 November 1817, had been to disseminate the knowledge of good English as widely as possible, so as to ensure that the 'whole body of the people' might become 'so completely capable of detecting and exposing the tricks and contrivances of their oppressors, that the power of doing mischief will die a natural death in the hands of those oppressors'.

Cobbett attributed slovenly grammar to moral laxity and combed the writings of Britain's statesmen and scholars for solecisms that could be taken as evidence of their corruptness and insincerity. Section XXIV of the *Grammar*, in which he demonstrates his great contempt for the prose of England's rulers, comprises six lessons which are quite explicitly 'intended to prevent statesmen from using False Grammar, and from writing in an awkward manner.' The examples are drawn from the speeches of Manners Sutton (Speaker of the House of Commons), the Prince Regent, Lord Castlereagh and the Duke of Wellington. Equally striking in its own way is the point being made by section XXI – one of the longest sections in the book – which consists entirely of 'specimens of false grammar, taken from the writings of Dr Johnson and from those of Dr Watts'. This systematic exposure of linguistic misbehaviour in the work of the 'Great Lexicographer' represents a real propaganda coup against what is perhaps the most significant eighteenth-century project of cultural conservatism.

Cobbett's English *Grammar* was not his first attempt at the genre; there had been an earlier book aimed exclusively at French émigrés to America who needed to acquire English as rapidly and efficiently as possible. The text had been developed out of Cobbett's experiences as a teacher of French refugees in Philadelphia, during his first residence in America between 1792 and 1800. *Le Tuteur anglais, ou Grammaire régulière de la langue anglaise* was first published in March 1795; it went into no fewer than 35 editions during the next 65 years. The author attributed its longevity and popularity to the fact that 'I myself always *reason*, and that I, thus, *induce the scholar to reason*: that I am not content with his *memory*, but force him to give me the use of his *mind*.'[11] This is a conscientious rejection of rote-learning, part of a determination to wrest the advantages of a knowledge of grammar out of the hands of a privileged few and make them available to a much wider spectrum of the population. The title page of the English *Grammar* announces that it is 'intended for the Use of Schools and of Young Persons in general; but, more especially for the Use of Soldiers, Sailors, Apprentices, and Plough-boys'.

The related issues of language and class, with a stress on the social harmony aimed at or projected by the philologists' interest in the history of language, are all touched on in the brilliant episode in Dickens's *Pickwick Papers* where controversy rages over the possible interpretations of a supposedly ancient inscription. Pickwick is the chairman of a 'corresponding society' whose members will have to travel to gain knowledge; he leads by example when he makes his 'immortal discovery, which has been the pride and boast of his friends, and the envy of every antiquarian in this or any other country.' The discovery is of an old stone, set in the roadway in the village of Cobham, which is uprooted at Mr Pickwick's request by a labourer living nearby who is prepared to affirm that 'it was here long afore I war born, or any on us.' Mr Pickwick's ecstasy at this discovery knows no bounds, especially after the stone has been cleaned, with the result that a 'fragment of an inscription was clearly to be deciphered':

+
BILST
UM
PSHI
S.M.
ARK

From this point on, the text indulges in a gleeful parody of the exhaustive analyses of comparative philology. The fragmentary inscription drives Mr Pickwick on to his greatest achievement: the composition of a pamphlet, 96 pages long, which contains no fewer than 27 different readings of the inscription. Other reactions apart from Mr Pickwick's include those of 'three old gentlemen [who] cut off their eldest sons with a shilling a-piece for presuming to doubt the antiquity of the fragment', and of 'one enthusiastic individual

[who] cut himself off prematurely, in despair at being unable to fathom its meaning.' Once the illegibility of the fragment has been confirmed by the sheer number of variant readings applied to it, the apparatus of commentary and interpretation becomes self-perpetuating:

> seventeen learned societies, native and foreign, being roused, several fresh pamphlets appeared; the foreign learned societies corresponded with the native learned societies; the native learned societies translated the pamphlets of the foreign learned societies into English; the foreign learned societies translated the pamphlets of the native learned societies into all sorts of languages; and thus commenced that celebrated scientific discussion so well known to all men, as the Pickwick controversy.[12]

What Mr Pickwick starts up, what is generated by his example, is a process of translation, even though the origin of these multiplying translations is quite precisely the mark of something unique, of an irreducible individuality that must remain ultimately untranslatable – because what is discovered by the egregious Mr Blotton, who interviews the labourer in question, is that the simple, linear reading of the inscription is best: 'BILL STUMPS HIS MARK.' The labourer who had vouched for the antiquity of the stone to Mr Pickwick, had not vouched for the antiquity of the inscription, which he had carved himself.

We are not given any of Mr Pickwick's 27 different readings of the inscription, but what we do learn is that his apprehension of brute reality is ingenuous, naive, credulous, laughable in some respects, but that it also represents a desire to promote understanding, to complete what is fragmentary, to repair what is broken, to restore what is lost. The members of the Pickwick Club express their admiration of him with a gift of gold spectacles, and the gift itself conveys the same tension of qualities; Mr Pickwick needs glasses because he cannot see what is staring him in the face, but at the same time this is perceived as something of a virtue – a gilt-edged defeat, so to speak – when it elevates the commonplace, romanticizes the sterile, harmonizes the discordant, translates the rustic into the genteel. Mr Pickwick lives in a world of societies: small communities of *savants* who collaborate in each other's researches and duplicate each other's views. Mr Blotton introduces a sour note of solitary, individualistic dissent. Moreover, he disrupts the aura of respectability that clings to the very idea of being a member of a learned society. The cast of Blotton's mind is 'vulgar' and 'degrading', and the reading he favours is a crude one: a triumph of near-illiteracy, irredeemably proletarian. Disruption, dissent and a brand of selfish individualism, then, are connected with an attack against that gentility of which Pickwick is such an extraordinary representative. If in so many other ways he is a clear descendant of the heroes of eighteenth-century picaresque novels, he is at least an early Victorian in the refinement and harmlessness of his appetites. It has often been noted how un-masculine Pickwick is, in conventional terms; his virtues are those which have been regarded traditionally as the feminine ones of giving, caring, healing.

Pickwick, with his carefully laid plans to introduce peace and harmony into the relations of those he encounters, can be taken to represent the best intentions of the philologists, of those who look to the history of the language as a source of stability and security in the social realm. Blotton, meanwhile, stands for the embattled outsider prevented from earning a position of advantage in society, or a chance of self-definition on his own terms, by an attitude towards language in which he recognizes the reality of a working-class speech that cannot be assimilated to a genteel standard. Between these two positions there lies the social arena of economic opportunism, of class rivalry and legalized injustice, where disagreements about linguistic form and meaning are set immediately within the context of a history of property-owning, of inherited values and affiliations, of institutionalized violence.

The high cost of linguistic nonconformism, and the kind of risk it involves is most strikingly embodied in the character of the irrepressible Jingle. Jingle represents the most ceaselessly effective resurgence of the principles that Blotton stands for. He perpetually reintroduces the note of disruption, of individual self-interest and of shrewdness. He even speaks in fragmentary inscriptions – jingles, rather – strings of nouns and adjectives delivered in a staccato manner almost totally devoid of verb forms. He is a master of disguise and deception, his every appearance marked by a change of costume, but he is always recognizable to the reader by his language, the recklessness and irregularity of his speech patterns being complemented by the substance of his anecdotes, with their images of alarming fracture:

> 'Heads, heads – take care of your heads!' cried the loquacious stranger, as they came out under the low archway, which in those days formed the entrance to the coachyard. 'Terrible place – dangerous work – other day – five children – mother – tall lady, eating sandwiches – forgot the arch – crash – knock – children look round – mother's head off – sandwich in her hand – no mouth to put it in – head of a family off – shocking, shocking!'[13]

Here again the black humour of the word-play revolves around a threat to the unity and coherence of a family tradition. Loquacity, of a kind which deviates strongly from the 'standard language', and marks one out as a 'stranger', is associated with mutilation and with breaks in the continuity of family history.

What is remarkable is how much the tone and method of the Dickensian narration owe an allegiance to the confidence tricks, fraudulence, exaggeration and sheer ridiculousness of Jingle. It reproduces the same high-energy spurts of invention not clearly connected; it puts all its verve into constructions which steer triumphantly away from coherence. And on that score it would seem that the book is subject to irreconcilable impulses of enthusiasm for the transparent honesty of Pickwick on the one hand, and for the outrageous deceptions of Jingle on the other. What Dickens is evidently repelled by are the methods of a social regime in which identity is created by a process of ruthless standardization.

One category of members of this society whose opportunities for self-realization are severely curtailed is that of women. In the decade after the publication of *The Pickwick*

Papers, there appeared a number of literary treatments of gender inequality, probably the most famous of which could be found in certain passages of Charlotte Brontë's novel *Jane Eyre*:

> Women are supposed to be very calm generally: but women feel just as men feel; they need exercise for their faculties, and a field for their efforts as much as their brothers do; they suffer from too rigid a restraint, too absolute a stagnation, precisely as men would suffer . . .[14]

Not since the time of Euripides, perhaps, had the representation of women's needs been so forthright, with the difference that Jane Eyre's protest is the work of a female, not a male author. Nonetheless, this complaint against the restrictions imposed on women in early Victorian society is mounted as part of an effort to emulate men, to enjoy their social advantages and to occupy masculine professional roles. The decision made by Charlotte, Emily and Anne Brontë to publish under the pseudonyms Currer, Ellis and Acton Bell in order to disguise their gender, indicates the limited extent to which women felt able to define themselves using any terms that valorized women's experience as distinct from men's. The attempt to inhabit the same social space as men, to think and feel in the same way and to speak the same language, actually confirmed and reinforced the effectiveness of male control over female lives. In Charlotte Brontë's first published novel, the devotion of the hero to the heroine is given a curiously selfish quality. Rochester's tenderness is seen as indistinguishable from his possessiveness; his desire to cherish Jane becomes equally a desire to bind and supervise her.

It is actually in the work of a male novelist, Thomas Hardy, that we hear one of the first powerful articulations of the view that a woman's experience could only ever be represented in language that does not reflect the standards of judgement or modes of awareness historically employed by men. In *Far From the Madding Crowd*, the heroine Bathsheba stresses how 'It is difficult for a woman to define her feelings in language which is chiefly made by men to express theirs'. It must be admitted that the narrator makes a related point about the hero, Gabriel, who 'would as soon have thought of carrying an odour in a net as of attempting to convey the intangibilities of his feeling in the coarse meshes of language'.[15] But the general concern to mark the inability of a standard language to deal with the needs and desires of unempowerered or dispossessed figures gathers strength particularly in those passages where gender is an issue.

In the early twentieth century, the recognition of an absent resource is converted into a plea for remedies, for the construction and use of a 'woman's sentence', for new forms of language enabling women to speak for themselves at last. Virginia Woolf provides the most cogent and impassioned appeal for new kinds of writing that will take the 'natural shape' of a woman's thought 'without crushing or distorting it'. In *A Room of One's Own*, she praises those women writers who have broken the moulds of both sentence and sequence: she evinces the work of Mary Carmichael who 'has every right to do both these things if she does them not for the sake of breaking, but for the sake of creating'.[16] The extremely complex nature of a female sensibility could only ever be explored by means of radical linguistic innovation; 'the resources of the English Language would be much put to the stretch, and whole flights of words would need to wing their way illegitimately into existence.'[17]

In her own work, Woolf associates maleness with rationalism of a sterile and reductive kind, with the aims and effects of control and regulation, while femaleness is linked to a fertile indiscipline, spontaneity, plenitude, a creative irrationalism. Among the more celebrated exemplars of these contrasting modes are Mr and Mrs Ramsey in *To the Lighthouse*, and Clarissa Dalloway and Dr Bradshaw in *Mrs Dalloway*. A more recent formulation of the contrast is to be found in the French theorist Julia Kristeva's distinction between the symbolic and semiotic poles in language. For Kristeva, normative grammar and conventional methods of making sense in language contribute to the formation of a 'symbolic order' which is what gives the individual subject a position from which to speak and relate to others. By definition, the reproduction of the symbolic order in language-use empowers the position of the male speaker, while the disruption of the symbolic order has the opposite effect. The symbolic order is constantly forged anew out of the linguistic material of the 'semiotic'. The semiotic is that which has not yet taken form; it is usually referred to as a set of impulses and drives that feed into language at a pre-semantic level. The semiotic encompasses everything that the normative excludes, as well as that which it reduces to order. The constant pressure it exerts on conventional form threatens to render provisional the relative positions of the symbolic order and so destabilize an essentially male conception of the world.

Another French theorist, the feminist Hélène Cixous, follows a comparable line, and argues the need to abandon linguistic mastery for the sake of reflecting the 'multiple nature of the self which can never simplify itself to conform to the illusion of its unified mirror image'.[18] In her view, it is through the grammatical subversiveness of poetic writing that one can hope to achieve the greatest degree of 'liberty taken inside language, with regard to the law of gender'. This identification, and celebration, of *écriture feminine*, or women's writing, effects a great historical reversal of the traditional strengths and weaknesses of male and female language-use. It gives a positive value to precisely those qualities that men have always derogated in women: hysteria, lack of force, sensitivity – all those qualities, in short, that Matthew Arnold enumerated as sure signs of the femininity of the Irish nation and the Celtic race. The simple reversal of positive and negative attributes is problematic if it keeps the same terms of definition found in men's language, even if it entirely revalues them, since it does nothing to create a new conception of women's experience. It works instead to essentialize the old notions of what makes women women, and what makes men men.

Moreover, Kristeva's observations on the tension between the symbolic and the semiotic cannot be reduced to the simple opposition of male and female principles, since the semiotic pre-exists and extends beyond the symbolic order, outside and before the phase, or area, where gender difference becomes significant. In sexual terms, the semiotic contains the potential for development of either masculine or feminine traits.

Empirical research into the speech patterns of contemporary women has shown such a degree of divergence from the models established by the traditional male/female axis that it seems more accurate to think of the language of women as no more nor less influenced by factors of race, class, education and wealth than that of men, except that a statistical average of women reflects a higher proportion of the factors of disadvantage than that of men, ensuring some degree of continuity with the stereotype of women's speech as hesitant, unassertive, lacking in emphasis and control.[19]

In short, although standard forms of language enshrine the history of power relations in which men have always succeeded in imposing their will on women, this is a state of affairs that will not be altered by a revolution in language alone. The recent controversies excited in the United States by the use of 'politically correct' terms in academic communities offer a case in point. Although the replacement of familiar terms such as 'history', 'mankind' and 'women', with their contraries, or negations, in 'herstory', 'humankind' and 'womyn', is clearly motivated by a progressive political agenda, it is equally clearly preparing the way for a new orthodoxy, with all the pitfalls of standardization that this entails. In some academic contexts, the monitoring of politically 'incorrect' discourse can lead to bans and boycotts whose effect seems out of all proportion to the cause. Aimed directly at combatting the disadvantages of minority groups within society as a whole, the application of ameliorative terms, such as 'people of color' in respect of Americans of African descent, is occasionally regarded by the subjects of this concern as in itself a political error that obliterates the most significant aspect of their social identity: consequently, some African Americans show determination in referring to themselves as 'black'.

The transformation of linguistic conventions may involve nothing more than, for example, replacing a generic 'he' with a generic 'she' – or the clumsier but more equitable 's/he' – or it may involve the more radical innovations of an avant-garde and experimental poetic. Either way, it can only ever be regarded as a preparation for social change, and an accompaniment to it, not as the central means by which it may be brought about.

CHAPTER SEVEN

THE DEBT TO MEANING: LANGUAGE AND MONEY

米要請に積極対応
防衛力増強で三原則
首相講演
外人記者クラブ

CHAPTER SEVEN

THE DEBT TO MEANING: LANGUAGE AND MONEY

No man but a blockhead ever wrote, except for money.
Samuel Johnson

From the moment that language began to be recorded, it was linked with economic media of exchange, and particularly with money. Writing may have come into being initially as a means of regulating trading deals (see chapter two). What is certain is that the introduction of inscribed metal coinage brought money and language into such close relations with each other that similar questions of meaning and value have remained a part of the history of each.

According to Greek tradition, the first ruler to mint coins was Gyges, one of the kings of Lydia. The other most notable achievement granted to this legendary figure was the invention of tyranny. If the move from tyranny to democracy was reflected in major shifts in Greek language-use, it must be no surprise if the inauguration of tyranny was accompanied by similar transformations. The link between tyranny and coinage makes conceptual sense, whether or not the stories about Gyges can be verified (they can't).

The elevation of the ruler to god-like status requires the establishment of conditions in which government is effected through a chain of command which removes the ruler to a position of aloofness and renders him inaccessible to the ordinary populace. For those who are asked to obey the commands transmitted along this chain, there must be some guarantee that the orders they are receiving actually originate from the ruler and not elsewhere. The authenticity of the royal command is therefore confirmed by symbolic means, chief among which are money and writing, although the use of symbols themselves can raise further doubts about the reality of something which remains invisible.

The process by which autocratic rule is established is most vividly evoked in Herodotus's account, not of Gyges but of Deioces, king of the Medes. According to Herodotus the huge social distance which is opened up between the ruler and the ruled is given physical expression in the construction of an elaborate system of concentric walls, made of different materials and painted different colours. Of great symbolic significance are the colour and construction of the innermost walls, which are of silver and gold, the final wall of gold encircling the royal palace and the treasury. The most precious material known to the community is reserved for association with royal privilege, and when minted as coinage it becomes the means of expressing the royal will. The image and name of the ruler on the coin is what validates both credit and exchange.

The most striking feature of coinage in respect of the history of language is that it anticipates some of the effects of printing two thousand years before Gutenberg's invention of the printing press. While writing was controlled by scribes in the intervening period, with the number of copies determined by the relative industriousness of any given scriptorium, in a pen-pushing version of sweatshop production, having the same inscription stamped onto thousands of metal discs represented the earliest form of publishing with a mass circulation. At the same time, the repetition of the royal or divine image on the face of the coin truly brought the work of art, even at this ancient date, into a distinctly modern age of mechanical reproduction.

If the image on the coin was utilized to begin with as a guarantee of value, the multiplication of the image was bound, in the long run, to produce something of the reverse effect. If each coin was equal in value to the next, and if the amount of money it stood for had the capacity for equalizing virtually everything in the social world, then the image of the

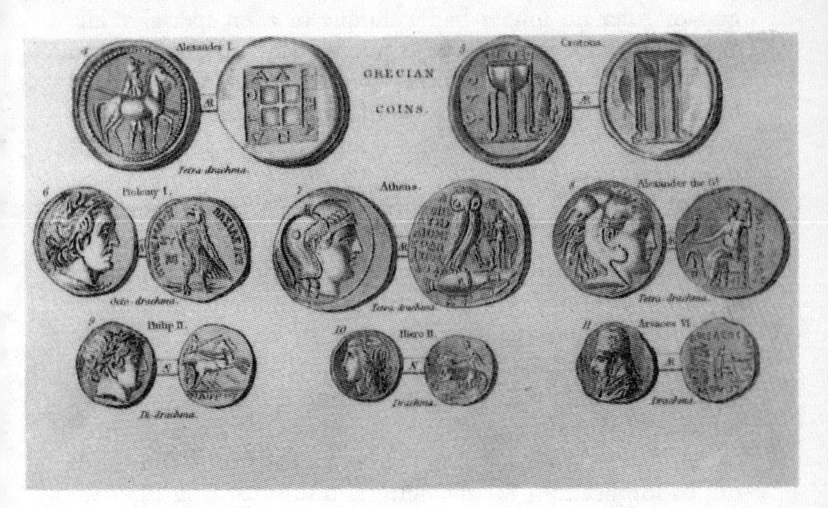

Ancient Greek coins with heads of rulers on obverse sides.

Universis Christifidelibus presentes litteras inspecturis Paulinus Chappe Consiliarius Ambasiator et procurator generalis Serenissimi Regis Cypri in hac parte Salutem in domino. Cum Sanctissimus in Christo pater et dominus noster dominus Nicolaus divina providentia papa quintus, Afflictioni Regni Cypri misericorditer compatiens, contra perfidissimos crucis Christi hostes, Theucros et Saracenos gratis concesserit omnibus Christifidelibus ubilibet constitutis, ipsos per aspersionem sanguinis domini nostri Jhesu Christi pie exhortando qui infra triennium a prima die Maii anni domini Mccccliii incipiendum pro defensione catholice fidei et regni predicti de facultatibus suis magis vel minus prout ipsorum videbitur conscientiis procuratoribus vel nunciis substitutis pie erogaverint ut Confessores ydonei seculares vel regulares per ipsos eligendi confessionibus eorum auditis pro commissis etiam Sedi apostolice reservatis excessibus criminibus atque delictis quantumcunque gravibus pro una vice tantum debitam absolutionem impendere et penitentiam salutarem iniungere Necnon si id humiliter petierint ipsos a quibuscunque excommunicationum suspensionum et interdicti aliisque sententiis censuris et penis ecclesiasticis a iure vel ab homine promulgatis quibus forsan innodati existunt absolvere. Iniuncta pro modo culpe penitentia salutari vel aliis que de iure fuerint iniungenda ac eis vere penitentibus et confessis vel si forsan propter amissionem loquele confiteri non poterint signa contritionis ostendendo plenissimam omnium peccatorum suorum de quibus ore confessi et corde contriti fuerint Indulgentiam ac plenariam remissionem semel in vita et semel in mortis articulo ipsis auctoritate apostolica concedere valeant. Satisfactione per eos facta si supervixerint aut per eorum heredes si tunc transierint Sic tamen quod post indultum concessum per unum annum singulis sextis feriis vel quadam alia die ieiunent legitimo impedimento ecclesie precepto Regulari observantia, penitentia iniuncta, voto vel alias non obstantibus. Et ipsis impeditis in dicto anno vel eius parte anno sequenti vel alias quam primum poterint ieiunabunt. Et si in aliquo annorum vel eorum parte dictum ieiunium commode adimplere nequiverint Confessor ad id electus in alia commutare poterit caritatis opera que ipsi facere etiam teneantur Dummodo tamen ex confidentia remissionis huiusmodi quod absit peccare non presumant Alioquin dicta concessio quo ad plenariam remissionem in mortis articulo et remissio quo ad peccata ex confidentia ut premittitur commissa nullius sint roboris vel momenti Et quia devotus frater Fridericus Schulem altarista in ecclesia S. Sebaldi Iuxta dictum indultum de facultatibus suis pie erogavit merito huiusmodi indulgentiis gaudere debet In veritatis testimonium Sigillum ad hoc ordinatum presentibus litteris testimonialibus est appensum Datum Neuremberge Anno domini Mcccclv die vero vicesima sexta Mensis Marcii

Forma plenissime absolutionis et remissionis in vita

Misereatur tui etc. Dominus noster Jhesus Christus per suam sanctissimam et piissimam misericordiam te absolvat Et auctoritate ipsius beatorumque Petri et Pauli apostolorum eius ac auctoritate apostolica michi commissa et tibi concessa Ego te absolvo ab omnibus peccatis tuis contritis confessis et oblitis Etiam ab omnibus casibus excessibus criminibus atque delictis quantumcunque gravibus Sedi apostolice reservatis Necnon a quibuscunque excommunicationum suspensionum et interdicti aliisque sententiis censuris et penis ecclesiasticis a iure vel ab homine promulgatis si quas incurristi dando tibi plenissimam omnium peccatorum tuorum indulgentiam et remissionem Inquantum claves sancte matris ecclesie in hac parte se extendunt. In nomine patris et filii et spiritus sancti Amen.

Forma plenarie remissionis in mortis articulo

Misereatur tui etc. Dominus noster ut supra Ego te absolvo ab omnibus peccatis tuis contritis confessis et oblitis restituendo te unitati fidelium et sacramentis ecclesie Remittendo tibi penas purgatorii quas propter culpas et offensas incurristi dando tibi plenariam omnium peccatorum tuorum remissionem. Inquantum claves sancte matris ecclesie in hac parte se extendunt. In nomine patris et filii et spiritus sancti Amen.

A Gutenberg typeface of 1455.

god or ruler no longer had a unique or even special value. What had once been the object of worship and respect had lost its aura. Money, in other words, grew into a crucial means by which the dislocation of meaning, the problematic relationship between signs and things, became an important social fact.

And if coinage introduces this kind of complication into the representation of meaning and value, the problems it raises are only further compounded by the way that paper money is expected to function in an economy. For most of the history of coinage, coins have contained precious metals, enabling them to function both as commodities and symbols. With the abandonment of precious-metal coins in favour of metal tokens and paper bonds the separation of the symbol from the commodity it denoted became absolute, and this is full of implications for the cultural history of language.

In an economy subject to a commodity law of values there are two basic perspectives on the law of exchange. In the first, a unit of money can be exchanged against goods of a certain value. From the second perspective, a unit of money is seen particularly in relation to all the other terms of the monetary system. The first perspective opens up onto exchange value, use value, and even 'natural' value, where the worth of a thing is thought to inhere in it naturally, and where wealth is measured in terms of the possession of things which have this 'natural' value, such as land and precious metals. David A. Wells, the American author of *The Silver Question: the Dollar of the Fathers versus the Dollar of the Sons* (1877) and *Robinson Crusoe's Money* (1896), states that the choice of gold as a measure of value has both a genealogical and an evolutionary inevitability; indeed, 'In civilized nations, natural selection has determined the use of gold as a standard'.

The second perspective on the law of exchange gives money a structural dimension, where what is being stressed is the interchangeability of all commodities according to a law of equivalence. With a structural law of values, the first perspective starts to disappear while the second perspective takes over. To take a few concrete examples, what exactly is the value of, say, a Filofax, a Porsche, or a stately home? Is it the amount of money one can get for each of these things, or does it have to do with the way they function within the social system as signs of status, taste or sophistication?

The operations of these different laws of value are important in the context of a discussion of language because there are parallels in the way that linguistic systems function. The first perspective in the operation of a money economy resembles the functioning of the referential dimension in language, whereby the most important relationship that any word can have is with what it refers to, what it designates. The picture is made clearer perhaps by the help of terms supplied by the Swiss linguist Ferdinand de Saussure. If we divide a linguistic sign for convenience into two components, signifier and signified, or word and concept, then the referential function becomes apparent when every signifier is related first and foremost to what it signifies, just as every piece of money refers to something against which it can be exchanged. With a structural law of value, this relationship is disturbed and sometimes deeply undermined. It is particularly the case with literary language that the referential function is no longer taken as the main goal in the range of its operation. Indeed, in certain modern literary texts, there is such an unusual stress on the need to release the signifier from its obligation to the signified, and to allow the language of the text a much greater degree of freedom to be drawn into structural play, that the linguistic signs start to be exchanged almost exclusively among themselves, without very much interaction at all with what they are supposed to refer to. Still, even such an extreme example as Joyce's *Finnegans Wake* maintains some degree of contact with the referential function, despite a primary stress on the multivalency of its puns. The possibilities and risks that arise when a structural law of value is dominant are universalized in societies whose economies are based on paper money. The extent to which earlier conditions of meaning-production are destabilized is suggested by Marx's dictum: 'Gold circulates because it has value whereas paper has value because it circulates'. Marx's contemporary, Dickens, recognized the extent to which language can be made to behave in a commodified manner in the very title of his travel book *American Notes for General Circulation* (1842).

The earliest paper money seems to been have developed in China. Marco Polo encountered it on his travels and tried to explain how it worked with reference to alchemy, but his European audience still failed to grasp the concept. Shakespeare's Richard II is credited with trying the experiment of issuing 'blank charters' and 'rotten parchment bonds'. The first trial run at basing a modern economy on paper money was engineered by John Law, the Scottish financier who founded the Banque Generale in France in 1716.[1] This institution did well for an initial period but foundered after four years.

It was a particularly significant time for the introduction of paper money. The difference between the French and English economies corresponded to divergent linguistic practices. In France, relative positions in the social hierarchy were marked in ways that were totally inapplicable on the other side of the Channel. Cultural prestige was identified with a rhetorically elaborate, even florid, form of speech that was enshrined as an objective in terms of national policy. A self-conscious classicism was placed at the centre of Richelieu's programme for the Académie Française, which had been founded in 1635. The Académie's task was to codify the French language and turn it into an appropriate instrument for the vast centralized bureaucracy of the absolutist state.

In Britain, the equivalent institution was pursuing a totally different policy. The Royal Society was chiefly concerned to promote a use of language that was instrumental to the new science being developed in fulfilment of Sir Francis Bacon's programme for the 'Great Instauration'. Bacon had denounced rhetorical excess and, in particular, the use of metaphors and other figures of speech: 'all that concerns ornaments of speech, similitudes, treasury of eloquence, and such like emptiness, let it be utterly dismissed.'[2] These recommendations were taken to heart so thoroughly that, by 1667, Thomas Sprat was able to record in his *History of the Royal Society* the promulgation of a language-use characterized by 'a close, naked, natural way of speaking; positive expression; clear sense; a native easiness; bringing all things as near Mathematical plainness as they can; and preferring the language of Artizans, Countrymen and Merchants, before that of Wits or Scholars.'

The last clause indicates the extent to which an economical use of language could be harmonized with the ethos of a society increasingly dominated by men of business. The preference for concision, a removal of waste, conformed with a rejection of the 'rentier mentality of non-utilitarian adornment and conspicuous consumption'.[3] What was to emerge as a typically English preference for plainness of speech, even for the laconic, matched a puritanical style of thought and feeling, responded to the pressures of a capitalist economy emphasizing productivity and profit, and became the vehicle of a uniquely English tradition of philosophical empiricism in which the referential function was paramount.

Just how closely, indeed intimately, the philosophical basis of this utilitarian attitude to language is meshed with the fortunes of the British economy, is brought out by the circumstances of the recoinage of the British money supply in 1696. The Master of the Mint on this occasion was Isaac Newton himself, while his closest colleague in the debate over methods of recoining was the most widely influential of the British empiricists, John Locke, author of *An Essay concerning Human Understanding*. The necessity for recoining had been brought about by an epidemic of coin-clipping that had been raging since the Civil War and had seriously debased the value of the currency. The ubiquity of clipped coins was such that the Treasury had begun to accept them into their accounts, which meant that the official distinction between clipped and unclipped coins ceased to exist. A huge proportion of the currency had lost its meaning; or rather a large number of coins no longer meant what they said they meant.

There were proposed two very different solutions to the problem in the 1690s, the first put forward by the Secretary of the Treasury, William Lowndes; the second by John Locke. Constantine Caffentzis has summarized these alternative methods: (1) take in the old coin at its 'face value' and return reminted coins with the same 'face value' but with about one-quarter less silver in every crown and shilling; (2) take in the clipped coin at weight and return a coin of the same weight, where crowns and shillings keep their old silver content.[4]

The result of adopting Lowndes's method would be to reissue the same number of coins, whereas the outcome of Locke's scheme would be the issue of fewer coins. Locke was concerned to preserve a *standard* of value. Fluctuation in the value of the standard, or rather the absence of a standard – since by its very nature a standard cannot fluctuate – allows the predominance of a structural law of value. Locke's philosophy of language works through similar issues. Those words which observe a standard of meaning are the names of substances that exist in nature, while those that drift away from a standard express a combination of ideas that cannot be correlated with natural substances. It follows that these 'mixed modes' are harder to translate from one language to another than are substance names, just as the currency of one state cannot be truly converted into the currency of another if either of them fails to maintain a standard (usually gold or silver), and introduces modifications to the commodity law of values. World trade, like universal languages, can only be achieved with difficulty as individual languages and currencies develop their own systems of relations.

The potentially demoralizing effect of constantly fluctuating standards is accentuated by the publication of bills that are not even, like banknotes, part of the currency (though that itself is subject to inflation and deflation), but stocks and shares, whose operation is predicated on a sliding scale of value. One of the most celebrated assessments of the damage this causes to human society can be found in the famous 'shares' passage of Dickens's *Our Mutual Friend*:

> The mature young gentleman is a gentleman of property. He invests his property. He goes in a condescending amateurish way, into the City, attends meetings of Directors, and has to do with traffic in shares. As is well known to the wise in their generation, traffic in shares is the one thing to have to do with in this world. Have no antecedents, no established character, no cultivation, no

> ideas, no manners; have Shares. Have Shares enough to be on Boards of Direction in capital letters, oscillate on mysterious business between London and Paris, and be great. Where does he come from? Shares. Where is he going to? Shares. What are his tastes? Shares. Has he any principles? Shares. What squeezes him into Parliament? Shares. Perhaps he never of himself achieved success in anything, never originated anything, never produced anything? Sufficient answer to all; Shares. O mighty Shares! To set those blaring images so high, and to cause us smaller vermin, as under the influence of henbane or opium, to cry out, night and day, 'Relieve us of our money, scatter it for us, buy us and sell us, ruin us, only we beseech ye take rank among the powers of the earth, and fatten on us!'[5]

The passage comprises a series of questions with corresponding answers. The questions, if answered properly, would make up the outline of a uniquely determined life, providing information about background and motivations, but each of the various questions is met with the same monotonous answer. A specific human complexity is reduced to the level of the lowest common denominator – exchange value – which is the only thing this character recognizes in himself and others, or is recognized for. The application of the principles of bargain and sale across the whole range of human activities works to eclipse the history that would otherwise have been the detailed and congested record of a highly specific adult life.

One particular striking aspect of this passage is that it contrasts the acquisition of shares with the accumulation of money. Share-dealing involves the 'scattering' of money, so that the dissipation of property is correlated with the loss of one's identity; the one is part of the same process leading to the other. This is a process of alienation rendering each individual interchangeable with all others. According to Locke, property is unthinkable without the action of memory, a form of control over time that leads ultimately to systems of patrimony and the establishment of laws of succession. This is why one of the most important functions of language for Locke is not to function as a system for exchanging ideas with others, but to provide a kind of memory bank for storing ideas for oneself and *of* oneself. Language becomes the chief means of ensuring continuity between past and present selves, of appropriating an identity. It is therefore no accident that the development of Locke's ideas coincides with the simultaneous rise in popularity of both the private account book and the diary.

Dickens reserves his greatest satire in *Our Mutual Friend* for his description of the market in orphans. His characters Mr and Mrs Boffin, who are searching for an orphan to adopt, uncover an endless supply of equally dispensable human units. They find that they have to thread their way through a minefield of 'genuine' and 'counterfeit' 'orphan-stock' and 'orphan scrip', and are perplexed by the fluctuations of a 'rigged' market:

> The suddenness of an orphan's rise in the market was not to be paralleled by the maddest records of the Stock Exchange. He would be at five thousand per cent discount out at nurse making a mud pie at nine in the morning, and (being inquired for) would go up to five thousand per cent premium before noon . . . fluctuations of a wild and South Sea nature were occasioned, by orphan-holders keeping back, and then rushing into the market a dozen together. But, the uniform principle at the root of all these various operations was bargain and sale . . .[6]

The point about orphans is that, in formal terms, they have no history; or rather, their relationship to memory, continuity, property, patrimony, and the laws of succession – and hence to identity – is severely inhibited simply because their parents have died. The constant hesitation over what is genuine and what is counterfeit – the loss of any external standard of meaning – is made possible by the relative blankness of the orphan, the relative lack of identity that is the mark of the automatically dispossessed.

Considerations like these form part of the reason why Dickens's use of language is so remote from that of the code of practice adopted and advanced by supporters of the Royal Society. Dickens recognizes that the only worthwhile identity in Victorian London – the only kind of identity that society as a whole will regard as valuable – depends on the possession of a certain amount of property. Failing to accumulate wealth is tantamount to failing to accumulate a personal history. If it is this kind of accumulation, this form of memory, that allows the maintenance of a standard of meaning, then Dickens is constantly at pains to measure the advantages and disadvantages, and to count the social costs of working to this kind of standard. That is why his language is so incurably playful and ambiguous, and why so often one can detect at least two horizons of meaning behind a single word or phrase. For example: about one third of the way through *Our Mutual Friend*, the character Mrs Wilfer, who is much less well-off than the Boffins, expresses her rather ridiculous sense of social superiority to them. The speech is addressed to one of her daughters:

> 'Mrs Boffin (of whose physiognomy I can never speak with the composure I would desire to preserve) and your mother, are not on terms of intimacy. It is not for a moment to be supposed that she and her husband dare to presume to speak of this family as the Wilfers. I cannot therefore condescend to speak of them as the Boffins. No, for such a tone – call it familiarity, levity, equality, or what you will – would imply those social interchanges which do not exist. Do I render myself intelligible?'[7]

It is possible to render Mrs Wilfer more intelligible than she is aware by registering the presence of one phrase standing behind another in the most interesting part of her speech:

familiarity, levity, equality,
fraternité, liberté, égalité

Dickens transforms phrases in this way all the time: he is unable to let sleeping words lie. He needs to reanimate dead bits of language, to resuscitate phrases which long usage has made almost meaningless. Dickens is resorting to the kind of ambiguity that Samuel Johnson found morally and politically so reprehensible for the threat it posed to linguistic tradition and cultural continuity. But Dickens recaptures a sense of the moment in which similar traditions and continuities were swept aside in the great social experiment of the French Revolution. The two horizons of meaning in Mrs Wilfer's phrase have the same kind of historical dimension implicit in Becky Sharp's opting to use Johnson's Dictionary for ballistics rather than linguistics. The first paradox of the passage is that Mrs Wilfer is made the defender of standards she feels are in danger of being undermined by the Boffins but which she herself symbolically undermines in an utterance that is semantically duplicitous. And the second paradox is that the standards she is foolishly trying to defend are those of a value system that prevents her from achieving any kind of social identity that the status quo would regard as worthwhile. The relocations of meaning and value that the French Revolution intended are exactly of the kind that would benefit impoverished figures like Mrs Wilfer. Dickens is aware of the disorientating effects of losing touch with tradition and being estranged from convention, but is also deeply suspicious of traditions and conventions that produce an experience of alienation for a majority of citizens. It is in the area of tension generated between a horizon of fixed standards and a horizon of no standards that the conditions of identity can be explored. Indeed, it is out of this tension that Dickens's highly idiosyncratic characters emerge, a tension that allows the reduction of human beings to units of exchange to be replaced by the irreducible foibles of the typical Dickensian eccentric. Although Dickens's work is carried forward on the energy created by this tension, he does not address the economy of language in any directly theorizing or self-conscious way. This task was in fact carried out at almost exactly the same time by John Ruskin, in *Munera Pulveris* (first serialized in 1862–3) and other writings. Ruskin considers language in the context of the production, distribution and exchange of books, and he considers books in the context of an analysis of the social value of art. The novelty of his approach is to regard not only art but also the artist as a kind of rare and therefore valuable resource, rather like a precious metal before it has been turned into coin. The test case for measuring the social value of art is offered by the goldsmith's and silversmith's art. In any society where gold and silver are given a higher value than artistic talent, the works of art made out of these metals will be melted down and the production of art made impossible. In a similar manner, literary books are regarded as repositories of a wisdom produced by an artistic use of language, and it requires the reader's aesthetic appreciation to recognize the value which has been added to the mere paper and ink.

An artistic use of language complicates the usual procedure by which language operates as a medium of exchange comparable to that of money. The reader of a book expects to be able to extract the knowledge of certain facts from its language just as a possessor of a banknote expects to be able to cash it in for a certain amount of silver or gold. In practice, such transactions seldom result in a yield of full meaning or value. Both the economic and the linguistic environments require fluidity or 'currency' in order to be kept in a healthily functioning state; both money and words need to be put properly into circulation and kept there in order for the media of exchange to operate successfully. In America, after the demonetizing of silver in 1873 had effectively halved the money supply, writers such as Ignatius Donnelly, in *The American People's Money* (1895), could claim that the 'Wall Street Misers' would be responsible for the return to another 'Dark Ages', by driving gold out of circulation. Any hoarding or excessive stockpiling, then, produces obstructions in the system: the secreting of money or words, miserliness or obscuration, prevents the smoothness of the transaction that enables the transfer of value or meaning. The converse of hoarding, profligacy or overspending – or an indiscriminate, uncontrolled use of words – entails miscalculations or inaccuracies, devaluation or the degrading of meaning:

> *The currency of any country consists of every document acknowledging debt, which is transferable in the country.*
>
> This transferableness depends upon its intelligibility and credit.[8]

Ruskin perceives how literary works are more likely than not to place obstructions in the way of intelligibility. Remarkably, he observes that the generation of literary works is almost proportional to the degree that they recognize the bar to intelligibility, the fallacy of treating language, along Royal Society lines, as a wholly transparent medium of exchange. Great works of literature suspect the impossibility of telling the truth about anything, and will even display the doubts they have about the viability of their own truth-telling acts. In conceiving of this economic basis for conditions of textual obscurity, Ruskin anticipates the grounds for a century or more of difficult literary experiments. His alternatives of hoarding and overspending answer to the tendencies of a great deal of ambivalent modern writing: to the cultivation of minimalist utterance, *poésie blanche*, the withholding of meaning on one hand; to the informational overload, paranoid superfluities, overprovision of meanings on the other.

Already in Joyce's *Ulysses* there is the recognition that the artist like Stephen Daedalus creates meanings for which there is no demand, while the advertising agent like Bloom creates demands for what has little meaning. But perhaps the most brilliant and systematic demonstration of how the production of meaning is controlled by a dynamic interaction of hoarding and overspending, or reticence and loquacity, is Conrad's *Nostromo*, whose story actually hinges on what happens to a miser's hoard of silver. In *Nostromo* the words that are most conspicuously put into circulation are, paradoxically, those that deal with the encrypting of meaning. And something similar happens in *Heart of Darkness* where, F.R. Leavis noted, Conrad makes annoyingly frequent use of words that deal with qualities of mysterious unintelligibility: 'unfathomable', 'inscrutable', 'impenetrable'. Leavis was identifying an important symptom without diagnosing the condition of which it was symptomatic.

What makes Conrad's economy of language so typical of the modern age has partly to do with his position as an exile. His relationship to language is that of a displaced cosmopolitan. Many of his best-known stories are concerned with the values that bind together small companies of men onboard ships. These are settings in which the problems of an economy, of a modern society with its infrastructures, can be suspended (although the pressure of keeping them out is often felt and takes it toll on the intelligibility of the text). Increasingly throughout the nineteenth and twentieth centuries, the experience of the émigré forced to cope with a second language has focused attention on how dependent the forms of a given language are on its social and cultural traditions. The questions that Conrad raises about how to determine what is 'genuine' and what 'counterfeit', are part of the ambivalent legacy of the émigré writing in a foreign language whose meanings he never fully managed to own, because he did not remember them as a part of his cultural 'property' and hence identity. The cultural obliquity of the émigré tests the limits and potential of any given set of traditional values.

At the same time as large-scale emigration was on the increase there was a shift in the understanding of how national character was linked to language and a move in the direction of exploring other and more sinister correlates. The stress on the importance of language as a factor of national unity was lifted to the degree that a greater stress was placed on the importance of sharing a history of being rooted in the same soil, or of sharing the same bloodstream. This proto-fascist outlook was bound to alienate Conrad and other exiles. Already in the first decade of the twentieth century, well-developed and profound misgivings about the scope and effectiveness of a common language were being fuelled by popular ideological pressures, and not just the personal circumstances of innumerable first-generation immigrants.

The rise of a global economy with its attendant marketing has given English, specifically American English, the status almost of a world language, just as the dollar has most often been used as a financial standard against which to value other currencies. In some economies, the symbolic power of the dollar has determined fluctuations in the value of key commodities. In Poland, throughout most of the 1980s it was the exchange rate of the złoty against the dollar that precisely determined the price of a bottle of vodka. The political structure determined by Soviet Marxism meant that Russian was the second language taught and learned in schools throughout the communist bloc. Yet the infiltration of the command economy by western marketing practices, and the consumer culture on which they were based, meant that English was the most prestigious and sought-after language in the countries of eastern Europe, a language given a value that could be starkly measured by the ability of English speakers to earn a living giving language lessons, a situation that was not available to those offering instruction in any other tongue.

The link between money and words, always important, has come to form an absolutely central strand in the fabric of modern society. In countries and economies where there is no money, the range of words available to describe the actions and agents involved in social transactions would seem to confirm they are living in a conceptual universe that is unrecognizable by modern capitalist standards. In the gift economies of Papua and Melanesia, researched by Marcel Mauss, it was possible for 'only a single word' to cover what seem to us the fundamentally different aspects of exchange covered for us by the words 'buy' and 'sell', 'borrow' and 'lend'. 'These men have neither the notion of selling nor the notion of lending,' recorded Mauss, 'yet they carry out the legal and economic activities corresponding to these words.'[9]

This demonstrates how the availability of words and concepts, and the mutual dependence of the two, can determine the scope not just of individual existences but of entire societies. It is in the nature of translation that these cultural restrictions on meaning give rise to some of the most problematic aspects of language.

CHAPTER EIGHT

THE CURSE OF BABBLE: THE LANGUAGE OF DISTRIBUTION

ᎾᏍᎩᎦᏃ ᏂᏕᎥᎩ ᎤᏁᎳᏅᎯ Ꭴ-
ᎰᏩᏒᎩ ᎡᏆᎯ, ᏕᎤᏂᏒᎩ ᎤᏙᏢᏕ Ꭴ-
ᏬᏂ ᎾᏍᎩ ᎤᎶᏒᎯᏩ ᎤᏕᏁᏄᎯ, ᎩᎶ
ᎾᏍᎩ ᏓᎪᎯᏩᏗᏍᏕ ᎤᏂᎱᎯᏍᏗᏜ ᏂᎦ-
ᏒᎾ, ᎬᏂᏳᏉᏍᎩᏂ ᎤᏩᏳᏗ.

CHAPTER EIGHT

THE CURSE OF BABBLE: THE LANGUAGE OF DISTRIBUTION

bababadalgharaghtakamminarronnkonnb-ronntonnerronntuonnthunntrovarrhounawnskawntoohoo-hoordenenthurnuk!

James Joyce, *Finnegans Wake*

The escalators in underground railway stations are popular places with advertisers. Here the potential consumers have nothing to do except stand, wait and look around while the moving staircase takes them up or down. The opportunity to display a range of advertisements is therefore irresistible, and the result can often be a welcome distraction, even a means of avoiding the gaze of other passers-by. Not long ago, all the available space alongside one of the escalators in a London underground station was taken up with the following letters: Y O U   C A N   T A K E   A   W H I T E   H O R S E   A N Y W H E R E. Most of those who glanced at this message would have understood how to read it, but not all would. For the majority of English readers, awareness of a previous advertising campaign would enable them to identify the product being recommended as a brand of whisky called 'White Horse'. The campaign itself had required the reader to use a modicum of linguistic skill by stressing the semantic ambiguity involved in calling a bottle of alcohol by the same name as an animal with four legs. A surreal effect had been the result of exchanging the literal for the figurative meaning in a series of photographic images placing white horses in situations where one might expect to find bottles of whisky instead. The reader had been required to perform an initial act of translation in reversing the process of literalization; and then a second kind of translation was needed when the images had to be retrieved from memory for the message alone to function in an appropriate way. These amusing obstacles in the way of intelligibility would have been frowned on by the Royal Society advocates of a 'naked, natural way of speaking', and would have been regarded as anathema by their most narrow-minded disciple, Dickens's Thomas Gradgrind. Chapter Two of *Hard Times* includes Gradgrind's famous invitation to Sissy Jupe, who spends her life among horses, to define the meaning of the word 'horse'. This she cannot do, and so the task is carried out by the monstrous Bitzer:

> 'Bitzer,' said Thomas Gradgrind. 'Your definition of a horse.'
>
> 'Quadruped. Graminivorous. Forty teeth, namely twenty-four grinders, four eye-teeth, and twelve incisive. Sheds coat in the spring; in marshy countries, sheds hoofs, too. Hoofs hard, but requiring to be shod with iron. Age known by marks in mouth.'[1]

Gradgrind then explains how wallpaper decorated with representations of horses should never be pasted onto walls, or, better yet, even conceived of, since in reality horses never do walk up, down, or across walls. In this respect, of course, it is his advice that has been quite precisely flouted by the manufacturers of White Horse whisky, whose images of horses are to be found on walls all over the place.

For anyone coming from a culture that had not been touched by this particular advertising campaign, the message by the escalator in the underground station would remain extremely puzzling. For anyone who had learned English in a culture other than England, it would be an easy enough matter to translate the literal meaning of the phrase, but extremely difficult to find the right context for it. It might seem most like a rather bizarre and irrelevant piece of practical advice. After all, in a public place like a railway station, one expects to see, and one does indeed see, several practical instructions. A purely linguistic translation would

A particularly elevated use of the White Horse whisky advertising slogan.

not be enough without a cultural translation as well. Even individual words in a phrase like this have connotations that are specific to one particular culture. The most important item of vocabulary in the phrase is 'white horse', which in English connotes 'a high white-crested racing wave' (*Oxford English Dictionary*). If one wanted to translate this particular connotation into French, one would have to resort to a completely different animal: a sheep. The equivalent word in French is *mouton*. In the French view of the world, the foam that runs before a moving wave resembles the curls of wool in a white sheepskin.

One might think that the choice of either sheep or horse is quite arbitrary and that the retention of different metaphors by these two cultures is the result of historical accident. But the white horse has another powerful connotation in English; tradition regards it as the ensign of the Saxons who invaded Britain, and the white horses cut into the chalk downs at Uffington, Berkshire, and elsewhere are held to be monuments of the Saxon victory. In this respect, the choice of horse, particularly a white one, as the basis for making metaphorical comparisons, is perhaps an intuitively English one to make, particularly since the Saxons were the invaders who came from the sea.

For a nomad coming from a culture based on the use of a horse, the message by the escalator would seem a perfectly natural statement to make. So natural, indeed, that it would hardly seem necessary to make a meal of it. Of course you can take your white horse anywhere; anywhere that is, apart from the kind of place where the message is actually located. A moving staircase would be the last thing to which you would think of introducing a horse or any other kind of animal. An underground railway station, in short, is among the very few places where such a message does *not* make much sense.

If the advertising slogan could be translated into Proto-Indo-European and shown to one of our ancient predecessors, he or she would be forced to conclude that nothing much has changed among our cultural priorities for many thousands of years. A Proto-Indo-European would also understand, without a moment's hesitation, the significance of the proverbial phrase: 'you don't look a gift horse in the mouth'. It would go without saying that a horse would be among the most precious gifts that anyone could ever receive. At the same time, one would know to gauge the value of any horse by looking in its mouth to estimate the age of its teeth. Historically, this basic 'horse sense' could have been found in every European culture until comparatively recent times. For the ancient Romans, certainly, there existed a Latin proverb whose sense was practically identical with the English one: *equi donati dentes non inspiciuntur* ('the teeth of a donated horse are not inspected'). Bitzer would have no trouble with the literal meanings of the words used in the slogan, and his definition of a horse would provide him with the necessary information for understanding why anyone should cast their gaze over a horse's teeth. But the whole point about Bitzer as a character in *Hard Times* is that his knowledge is divorced from experience; he has learned everything from books, not from life. 'Horses' are facts and figures to him, not living flesh and blood. This means he is a master, of sorts, of linguistic translation, but hopeless at the cultural equivalent. Dickens portrays him as a moral amputee; he has never had anything to do with horses, and he has problems with the idea of giving as well.

Not everyone turns out a Bitzer. But in a period of rapid technological change, it is true enough that a very important layer of meaning in the proverb has become rather thin and indistinct to the majority of its users today. In a largely urban environment, where most people move around with the help of mechanical contrivances – escalators included – 'horse sense' is an almost insignificant part of the culture: whisky is more familiar. Contemporary English children would understand the proverb less well in their native language than an ancient Roman who had been given a version in a Latin translation. The historical and geographical variables involved in the art of translation can be infinitely complicated, but it is certainly the case that cultural dislocation can present more barriers than any amount of linguistic difficulty. For this reason, one might say that 'you *cannot* take a white horse anywhere', because the problems of translation are too great.

Translation is at once the crucial facilitator of contact between cultures and the ultimate stumbling block to real understanding between one culture and another. Studies of bi-lingualism have shown the extent to which even the same mind and sensibility, equally adept in at least two languages, has difficulty in, and sometimes has to admit the impossibility of, translating the concepts of one culture into the words of another. Sometimes the problem is one of lexical inequality between one language and another; the number of words for snow, for example, available in Finnish but unavailable in Arabic; or the number of words to describe the behaviour of camels, available in Arabic but unavailable in Finnish. At other times, there are structural inequalities between languages which prevent the speaker of one sharing the same experience of time, location or relationship available to another.

In Polish, for example, verbs have no real future tense. A Polish verb, however, has a system of aspects, perfective and imperfective (these are not the same as perfect and imperfect tenses in other languages). For every English verb, there are these two corresponding aspects in Polish. What is perhaps confusing is that the difference between aspects is not necessarily marked by a difference of conjugation. Take, for example, the perfective (zobaczyć) and imperfective (widzieć) aspects of the verb 'to see':

	1. widzę	1. zobaczę
SINGULAR	2. widziesz	2. zobaczysz
	3. widzie	3. zobaczy
	1. widziemy	1. zobaczymy
PLURAL	2. widziecie	2. zobaczycie
	3. widzą	3. zobaczą

Both are conjugated as if for the present tense; and yet *zobaczyć* is commonly used to denote an action in the future. The distinction between aspects is marked not by conjugation but by lexical means alone. This makes it difficult for anyone learning the language not to say 'I will see' without thinking 'this is in the present tense', or to employ both aspects without thinking 'these words must refer to two different kinds of action'. At one level it is easy to translate *widzę* as 'I see', and *zobaczę* as 'I will see,' but at another level, the structure of Polish engenders a distinctive frame of mind with regard to temporal relations that the translation does not hint at.

The specific structure of each language, and the cultural context which controls the flow of meaning into and out of its words and phrases, combine to bring down the level of what is translatable from one language into another. The sheer inconvenience of translation is such that certain national languages have been used internationally as a means of cultivating trading and diplomatic links between states. In the ancient and medieval world, this role was performed most obviously by Greek and Latin; in the modern world by French, Russian and English. The emergence of these international languages has frequently coincided with the military, political or economic pre-eminence of the states originally associated with them. Even where this has not been the case, the customary use of a foreign language, in however limited a way, renders the culture of a client state permeable in some degree to the culture of the state it depends on.

In the process, a threshold is reached beyond which certain aspects of an original culture remain untranslatable. When that threshold is crossed, there may be a case for preserving intact the 'core' or unique elements of the culture, despite the fact that an alien language is being used for most of the purposes of everyday life. Alternatively, the 'core' elements may be supplemented by alien equivalents brought in with the language of the invader, or of the politically or economically dominant state. These different possibilities are at stake when there is 'language death', which is one of the most startling phenomena of all in the complex history of language. It remains a puzzle why certain so-called 'dead' languages like Latin manage to survive, even when the cultures associated with them have died out, while other languages disappear even though the people and cultures that once used them live on. Some of the best examples of the latter can be found within the British Isles in the various stages of decline, and sometimes artificial revivals, of the languages of Cornish and Welsh.

One may say that the use of an international language automatically introduces inequality into international relations. But even in situations where one language is not given a dominant role to play, and where each party makes a conscientious attempt to translate the language of the other, it is inevitable that the search for common ground should lead to a corruption of vocabulary. If translation is made the governing factor in the process of deciding which meanings are relevant and which are not, the result can be a dramatic change, first in the way we speak, and inevitably also in the way we feel and think. Everyone has had the experience, when using a foreign language, of finding certain words more 'international' than others; the word 'international' itself is a good example of this: in French, it is 'international': in German, 'international': in Spanish, 'internacional': in Italian, 'internazionale', and so on. But the facility with which words like this move among languages should make us cautious about using them. It may be that different nations give different meanings to these international words, while enjoying the illusion that everyone has the same meanings in mind. As George Orwell long ago pointed out, this is likely to be the case above all in respect of political vocabulary:

> The word *fascism* has now no meaning except in so far it signifies 'something not desirable'. The words *democracy*, *socialism*, *freedom*, *patriotic*, *realistic*, *justice*, have each of them several different meanings which cannot be reconciled with one another. In the case of a word like *democracy*, not only is there no agreed definition, but the attempt to make one is resisted from all sides. It is almost universally felt that when we call a country democratic we are praising it: consequently the defenders of every kind of régime claim that it is a democracy, and fear that they might have to stop using the word if it were tied down to any one meaning. Words of this kind are often used in a consciously dishonest way. That is, the person who uses them has his own private definition, but allows his hearer to think he means something quite different.[2]

In the more than four decades that have elapsed since Orwell wrote these words, his point has been borne out several times over. If we now ask, which was the more 'democratic', the German Democratic Republic, or the Democratic Party in the United States, we are rehearsing the same concerns.

One means of tackling, or perhaps getting round, the problems of translation, apart from the habitual use of an 'international' vocabulary or the use of an existing language as an international medium, is the creation of an artificial language for international communication. The most celebrated of all such experiments was (and is) Esperanto, devised by the Polish oculist Ludwig Zamenhof. Esperanto draws heavily upon all the main Romance and Germanic languages, although it also includes elements of Greek and of several slavonic languages. Its grammar is perfectly regular and comparatively simple. It aims to be impartial in its reliance upon the vocabularies of existing languages, yet its word order closely follows that of English. As many as fifteen million people are able to speak Esperanto today; nevertheless, it is scarcely ever used for practical purposes, and is mostly acquired by those who are interested in it for its own sake. Esperanto is a synthetic language composed virtually on statistical principles. In one sense, its least attractive feature is that it is so well planned. The ambitions of Zamenhof and his followers seem naive in retrospect, although there is no reason to doubt the idealism of their attempts to universalize the principles and practice of language in such a schematic manner. The planning of a language, however, leads ultimately to the planning of human sensibilities. What seems idealistic in conception may be realized in ways that alter or even betray the original design. In fiction, George Orwell's Newspeak, the language of *1984*, offers the most chilling anticipation of the kind of moral numbness that may result when natural languages are systematically 'purified' to remove all irregular and inconvenient elements:

> The purpose of Newspeak was not only to provide a medium of expression for the world-view and mental habits proper to the devotees of Ingsoc, but to make all other modes of thought impossible.[3]

Even if Esperanto is a failed or incomplete experiment, the lesson it has to teach about the value of what can be lost in the search for the lowest common denominator of reproducible sound and meaning is not without relevance for a Europe which is fast approaching various kinds of political and economic union and which will not be able to escape some degree of linguistic common cause. The kind and degree of translatability that comes in the wake of 1992 is of major concern. Even while governments consider ways of dealing with increasing amounts of federalism, the politics of popular action cut across international development programmes with expressions of sharply nationalistic loyalties and resentments. The expansion of a global economy coincides with the renewal of ethnicity and of local cultural identities; both tendencies bend and distort everyday speech in profoundly disturbing ways.

The most prominent form of language mutation occurs in war-time. Orwell's essay 'Politics and the English Language' is at once a reaction to the ideologically charged military jargon of the second world war, as well as empirical research into the possibilities of Newspeak. During his continuous lament over the degeneration of English, Orwell is scandalized more than by anything else by the obscene euphemisms of political spokesmen:

> Defenceless villages are bombarded from the air, the inhabitants driven out into the countryside, the cattle machine-gunned, the huts set on fire with incendiary bullets: this is called *pacification*. Millions of peasants are robbed of their farms and are sent trudging along the roads with no more than they can carry: this is called *transfer of population* or *rectification of frontiers*. People are imprisoned for years without trial, or shot in the back of the neck, or sent to die of scurvy in Arctic lumber camps: this is called *elimination of unreliable elements*.[4]

Each successive war modulates and expands this vocabulary. The cruelly paradoxical use of the term 'pacification' to refer to acts of brutality and destruction became routinized during the Vietnam war, as a means of making the colossal B-52 bombing raids seem relatively acceptable. Michael Herr's book, *Dispatches*, an account of the traumatic effect the Vietnam war had on members of the sixties generation, focuses constantly on the inadequacy of the official and journalistic descriptions of front-line experience, and makes a direct connection between the lack of authenticity in representations of the war and the psychological repercussions of undercover political activity on the part of the CIA. The 'spooks', as they were known, manufactured a constant supply of linguistic evasions, a 'jargon stream thinning and trickling out: *frontier sealing*, *census grievance*, *black operations* (pretty good, for jargon), *revolutionary development*, *armed propaganda*.'[5] More recent conflicts, such as the Gulf War of 1991 and the civil war that has followed the break-up of Yugoslavia, have involved a progressive indulgence in military–political 'translationese' whose misrepresentations are more and more blatant. There is now almost no attempt to deceive with this kind of language, since its deceptiveness is obvious to everyone: it is used instead as an act of defiance. The Serbian fondness for the phrase 'ethnic cleansing' to indicate what is no more nor less than a campaign of genocide is simply a lurid demonstration of the power that language has to define reality. Our awareness of what is happening in Bosnia is controlled by the kinds of language, verbal and visual, that are being used to report on and represent a clash of different cultures. Our suspicions of a gross disparity between the misery actually suffered by Bosnian Muslims and the assumption built into the phrase that murder and dispossession should be regarded as aspects of a bizarre kind of hygiene do not change the fact that the more powerful side in this struggle has achieved some success in the war of representations. The sheer audacity of the phrase 'ethnic cleansing' has given it a kind of disgusting attractiveness to the media. Its currency is such that it will remain as one of the principal emblems of its period, qualifying the historical memory to a degree that will colour the perceptions not only of those with no personal memory of the civil war, but also of those who have lived through the period in question, and who think they remember something different.

This is not a wild claim; it projects a situation easily matched in the history of reactions to the Second World War. Tom Harrisson's study *Living Through the Blitz* reveals the extent to which personal memories of an event can be displaced by rival versions composed in and by the language of published accounts. Harrisson was one of the founders of Mass Observation, a social-research movement whose data were provided by teams of observers recording their own individual responses to given events or living conditions in Britain from the late 1930s onwards. The archive of personal records provides the basis for comparison of immediate and subsequent reactions to the same events and conditions. With regard to the war-time Blitz, a majority of mass observers proved to have faulty memories when their initial and subsequent accounts were compared, and in the majority of cases the change of mind reflected a gravitation towards the publicly available and commonly shared view of what had taken place. Harrisson calls this process of adjustment 'glossification' and gives numerous examples like the following:

> Over in Stepney, the girl who was playing the piano and missed Chamberlain's words or the first siren on 3 September 1939 . . . completely transforms those events in memory. Then her mother burst in, shouting at her to stop playing, until Father took over, issuing dictatorial demands and unnecessary advice. Now she writes in recall: 'We were gathered in our little living room and it was very crowded, with the six of us (parents and four children) all together for once. But weren't there also visitors? I have the notion that this was a special kind of gathering, something a bit formal: aunts, uncles or neighbour, perhaps, all listening to the wireless, which, those days, was on almost all the time, in anticipation of more bad news. A vigorous discussion followed Chamberlain's speech (she remembers.) Then suddenly the siren. She is 'shaken to the roots' – in fact, she never heard it.[6]

There is almost no overlap between the contemporaneous and retrospective versions. What the girl of 1939 now 'remembers' is nothing she saw or heard on 3 September but a stereotypical scene of the kind familiar from newsreel footage covering Chamberlain's fateful broadcast. It is particularly significant that the language of a personal record has been completely obliterated by the authority of the public account. But it is also important that Harrison was able to retrieve what was originally written down in order to bear witness to this psychological compliance. When we relinquish our hold on the language we use, we relinquish our hold on the entire shape of our lives. The existence of the Mass Observation script is a reminder of how writing, because of its orientation towards memory as much as towards communication, provides some guarantee against our having words put into our mouths, and makes us think about the modes of knowledge that language introduces to our brains.

If the translations or transmutations of language outlined above produce feelings of alienation proportional to the ideological pressures apparent in contemporary language-use, these feelings must be equalled and compounded by the steady growth of interconnections between language and technology. The most significant advance in modern communications after the development of the printing press was the invention of the telephone system. The impact of the telephone on self-expression and dialogue, on the relations of the voice, sincerity and identity are incalculable. Speech is no longer identifiable with presence, yet the speed with which electronic signals can be transmitted allows the simulation of presence over vast distances. Electronic speech renders unnecessary the writing down of the majority of messages that need to be communicated, yet the lack of a transcription of what is said in a telephone conversation diminishes the level of answerability for the language that is used. The telephone summons its interlocutors with the sound of an alarm and gives no warning of the kind or duration of the message it is ready to convey. There is no defence against the telephone for those who cannot or will not deprive themselves of the knowledge it brings. It is a tool, yet it makes human beings instrumental to its functioning. Its appendage, the answering machine, has a playback facility which renders the telephone dialogue unequal, subjecting the first speaker to delay and suspense, amplifying the inefficiencies and hesitancies of the voice unsupported by physical gesture. The contemporary phenomenon of the 'phone-in' employed in television and radio programmes feeds the illusion of self-realization in the context of media that operate as a distraction from print culture. The latter still offers an occasion for exploring the conditions for modern selfhood that is much subtler and much fuller than in any medium devised by modern technology itself.

Much more disturbing than telephone culture, which now seems completely natural to us, is the language environment that has accompanied the growth of information-processing machines. What the computer effects, particularly when it is employed, as it increasingly is, in various types of learning process, is a constant translation of knowledge into measurable terms. 'Technobabble' and 'computerspeak' cannot be simply dismissed (however nervously) or quietly put in their place by individual human subjects who think they know better. As Jean-François Lyotard warns, in his seminal text *The Postmodern Condition*, a 'report on knowledge' prepared for the Conseil des Universités of the government of Quebec:

> We may thus expect a thorough exteriorization of knowledge with respect to the 'knower', at whatever point he or she may occupy in the knowledge process. The old principle that the acquisition of knowledge is indissociable from the training of minds, or even of individuals, is becoming obsolete and will become ever more so.[7]

Lyotard places the new information technologies at the centre of an emerging social reality in which he foresees that the only kinds of knowledge to survive will be those amenable to translation and to processing as information. Control of information will decide the balance of powers as the possession of territory did in the past, while nation states and national cultures will become increasingly anachronistic. 'Translatability' is inimical to Lyotard because his understanding of social interactions is governed by the terms of Wittgenstein's ideas about 'language games', according to which everything we say belongs to one or another category of utterance, but never to more than one category. Every speaker or listener is a player in a game whose rules do not apply in any other games. For example, the criterion of what is just or unjust, as used in the language game of prescription, cannot be used in a technological or scientific language game, where the criterion refers not to justice but to efficiency. This has important repercussions for ideas about contemporary selfhood; the speaker in a number of games can never occupy a unitary position in respect of a set of games. Rather, it is the games 'that make us into their players, and we know therefore that we are ourselves several beings.'[8] The social reality that is formed under these constraints is not unified but pluralized – it is a plurality of games – while the realm of politics is not one of consensus but of divergent attitudes, where a majority viewpoint is always absent because every citizen belongs to several minorities, none of which prevails over the others.

This is essentially the condition that has been identified as 'postmodern'. It has succeeded an earlier stage in the history of the West in which the social bond was derived not from the rules of a plurality of language games, but from the rules of narrative. Narrative is seen as the main way in which earlier societies produced assimilation between categorical statements about justice, efficiency, truth, beauty, and so on. Narrative provided the key models of relationship and intelligibility. Its predominance over other forms of knowledge is thought to have ended with the modernization of science and the power exerted by scientific discourse in its allocation of value to statements carrying out the work of denotation and proof. The struggle between narrative knowledge and scientific knowledge contained, however, a paradox, in that scientific knowledge could not establish its cultural legitimacy without making use of a narrative mode of discourse, without presenting its claims in the form of an ideology.

According to Lyotard, the two most important resulting 'grand narratives' stem from the French and German traditions of modernity: the first in pursuit of the revolutionary goals of liberation and equality, the second in connection with the Hegelian project of the unification of all branches of knowledge. With the evaporation of confidence in the projects of modernity, with the loss of belief in the idea of progress, the narrative form has entered a redundant phase. The development of technology has become inseparable from the functioning of a capitalist economy, with scientific research in the main depending on investment made possible by demonstrations of improved performance, which in turn can only result from technological advance. Under these conditions, science supposedly turns away from the pursuit of truth and in the direction of increased efficiency; the modernizing programmes of emancipation and totality become superfluous to the more urgent contemporary demand for utility. In an educational context, this builds up pressure behind the insistence on 'translatability', and behind the tendency to collate as information the research of different kinds of knowledge. Lyotard's recommendation is to exploit the interval between the decline of narrative and the supremacy of computers as an opportunity to reassess the social and political dimensions of language games. Although he welcomes the disappearance or erosion of 'grand narratives', he would still like to keep open the channels of communication between different language games by promoting the education of imaginative skills that would allow the player of a game to learn, from the differences between discourses, how to plan new moves or even how to invent new sets of rules. In other words, Lyotard would like to recover certain conditions of narrative but on a different scale – on the scale of individual strategies, not of collective projects.

What are the practical effects of translating the concerns of a natural language into the equivalent terms of a computer language? In contemporary written English, the number of words in an average sentence is about twenty, while in standard programming jargon the average would be half a dozen. The average number of grammatical rules according to which the sentences of a computer language are constructed is little more than 100, as compared to the thousands that are available and that are continually represented in contemporary usage. A fundamental reduction of scope and expressive power in the effective functioning of a natural language is not the inevitable outcome of a sustained exposure to computer usage, but it is obviously increasingly likely with the growth in computer literacy. For many students nowadays, being introduced to a subject of study may well be directly correlated with a means of processing data that discourages, rather than encourages, an individual ability to give a shape to their knowledge. This is one form of standardization that clearly answers to the aspect of cultural degradation hinted at in the title of this book. Paradoxically, exposure to technobabble invites a resumption of the state of artificial unanimity anticipated by the builders of that tower whose destruction mythically inaugurated the creative babble of human history.

Meanwhile, in its evolutionary descent, language has become inextricably meshed with the codes of information processing to a degree that makes less and less distinction between technological and vital structures and processes. On the one hand, there is a register in which the difference between 'hardware' (mechanical equipment) and 'software' (programmes) is neither more nor less apparent than either's difference from 'liveware' (human beings). On the other hand, a program that is capable of moving from one computer to another, disrupting files and deleting memories on the way, is given a biological rather than a mechanical name. To call such a program a 'virus' is to correlate technology with natural history, and thus make the capacities and vulnerabilities of computer operations seem more easily identifiable with the human sphere. This partly achieved, partly proposed, coexistence of natural and artificial languages has several depressing aspects, but the history of language-use has shown what resources we have to deal with it.

We have to take into account warnings like those issued by Lyotard; his 'report on knowledge' includes an extremely useful and provocative analysis of the long-term effects of information-processing on our language and experience. However, it underestimates the extent to which other factors, not least the categories of race, gender, class and nation, continue to govern our social relations and determine our cultural values. The politics of language demand an adaptability towards both individual strategies and collective projects; above all it requires a medium in which each alternative can be tested by the other's criteria. Both ideology and technology have a tendency to 'translate' knowledge into standard terms. It is only in literary writing that we already have a medium subtle enough, and complex enough, to bring the traces of special languages, special modes of knowledge together in one place for realizing the grounds of their incongruity. The reader of literature, and particularly of poetry, is drawn into a realization of the reduced range of choices that any 'translation' of knowledge incurs. Whatever special language is used to make sense of the world, it is only ever operational within a limited scope. It seems, on the evidence, that writing must refuse the latest version of standardization if it is to make more than a start in urgently questioning those structures of knowledge we are now confined to by the descent of language.

Introduction

1 Edward Sapir, *Language: an Introduction to the Study of Speech* (Rupert Hart-Davis, London, 1949)
2 William Golding, *The Inheritors* (London: Faber, 1955), p. 33.
3 Russell Hoban, *Riddley Walker* (London: Jonathan Cape, 1980), p. 6.
4 James Joyce, 'The Dead', from *Dubliners* (Harmondsworth: Penguin, 1956), p. 220.
5 Rev. John O'Rourke, *History of the Great Irish Famine of 1847* (Dublin, 1875), p. 15. See also Hon. Emily Lawless, *The Story of Ireland* (London: T. Fisher Unwin, 1888), p. 396.

Chapter One

1 Antonio R. Damasio and Hanna Damasio, 'Brain and language', *Scientific American*, vol. 267, no. 3 (Sept. 1992), p. 70.
2 Eugen Bleuler, *Dementia praecox or the group of schizophrenias* (New York: International University Press, 1950), p. 293.
3 Anonymous, 'In adoration of Nature the morning pawn 10th & 11th October 1976', in Rod Mengham and John Wilkinson (eds), *Equofinality*, no. 2 (1984), p. 14.
4 Marjorie Wallace, *The Silent Twins* (Harmondsworth: Penguin, 1987), p. 3.

Chapter Two

1 Ferdinand de Saussure, *Course in General Linguistics*, tr. Roy Harris (London: Duckworth, 1983), p. 29.
2 Aristotle, *De Interpretatione*, tr. H.R. Cook (London: Loeb, 1938), p. 115.
3 Saussure, op. cit. p. 24.
4 Plato, *Phaedrus and Letters VII and VIII*, tr. Walter Hamilton (Harmondsworth: Penguin, 1975), pp. 96–7.
5 ibid., p. 97.
6 Jacques Derrida, *Positions*, tr. Alan Bass (Chicago, 1981), p. 22.
7 American spelling practice often differs from English for the sake of removing such inconsistencies. American has *plow* rather than *plough*.
8 S. Sasanuma, 'Acquired dyslexia in Japanese: clinical features and underlying mechanisms', in M. Coltheart, K. Paterson and J.C. Marshall (eds), *Deep Dyslexia* (London: Routledge & Kegan Paul, 1980), pp. 48–90.
9 D. Schmandt-Besserat, 'The earliest precursor of writing', *Scientific American*, vol. 238, no. 6 (June 1978), pp. 38–47.
10 Homer, *The Iliad*, tr. Robert Fagles (London: Penguin, 1990), p. 201.
11 Walter J. Ong, *Orality and Literacy* (London: Methuen, 1982), chapter 4.
12 Herodotus, *The Histories*, tr. Aubrey de Selincourt (Harmondsworth: Penguin, 1954), pp. 331–2.
13 List compiled by B.B. Powell, in his *Homer and the Origin of the Greek Alphabet* (Cambridge University Press, 1991), p. 11.
14 I.J. Gelb, *A Study of Writing* (Chicago: University of Chicago Press, 1963), p. 165.
15 *The Iliad*, p. 317.
16 'A *foot* is the combination of a strong stress and the associated weak stress or stresses which make up the recurrent metric unit of a line.' M.H. Abrams, *A Glossary of Literary Terms* (6th edn, Fort Worth: Harcourt, Brace, Jovanovich, 1993), p. 113.
17 Herodotus, *The Histories*, p. 332.
18 The cultural implications of this love affair between the alphabet and literature finds a negative reflection in the regressiveness of the Etruscans, who had no interest in literature and reverted to syllabic writing even after they had learned how to use the alphabet. Perversely, they continued with their own version of the Euboean alphabet, but only after scrupulously shedding it of all its vowels.

Chapter Three

1 Stephen Rodefer, *Four Lectures* (Berkeley, California: The Figures, 1982), p. 9.
2 Quoted in J.P. Mallory, *In Search of the Indo-Europeans, Language, Archaeology and Myth*

(London: Thames & Hudson, 1989), p. 12.
3 Colin Renfrew, *Archaeology and Language; the Puzzle of Indo-European Origins* (London: Jonathan Cape, 1987).
4 James Parsons, *The remains of Japhet, being historical inquiries into the affinity and origins of the European Languages* (London, 1767).
5 Herodotus, *The Histories*, pp. 102–3.
6 ibid., pp. 243–4.
7 Mohammed Khalifa, *The Sublime Qur'an and Orientalism* (London: Longman, 1983), p. 219.
8 See Michael Baigent and Richard Leigh, *The Dead Sea Scrolls deception* (London: Jonathan Cape, 1991) and R.H. Eisenman, *Maccabees, Zadokites, Christians and Qumran* (Leiden: E.J. Brill, 1983).

Chapter Four

1 Simon Goldhill, *Reading Greek Tragedy* (Cambridge University Press, 1986), p. 235.
2 Plato, 'Gorgias', in Benjamin Jowett, *The Dialogues of Plato* (3rd edn, Oxford University Press, 1892), 515E.
3 Jean-Pierre Vernant and Pierre Vidal-Naquet, *Myth and Tragedy in Ancient Greece* (Brighton: Harvester, 1981), p. 18
4 Sophocles, *The Theban Plays*, tr. E.F. Watling (Harmondsworth: Penguin, 1947), p. 66
5 Goldhill, op. cit., p. 217.
6 William Shakespeare, *Macbeth*, I. iv. 27–9, ed. Kenneth Muir (London: Methuen, 1972), p. 24.
7 *Macbeth*, I. ii. 22–3, ed. cit., p. 7
8 *Macbeth*, IV. iii. 216–21, ed. cit., p. 139.
9 Bertolt Brecht, *The Messingkauf Dialogues*, tr. John Willett (London: Methuen, 1965), p. 63.
10 *Macbeth*, V. iii. 25–6, ed. cit., p. 152.
11 I am thinking of the title of a particularly influential book on the literature, life and ideas of this period, Stephen Greenblatt's *Renaissance Self-fashioning* (University of Chicago Press, 1980).
12 Shakespeare, *King Lear*, II. iv. 54, ed. Kenneth Muir (London: Methuen, 1952), p. 85.

Chapter Five

1 Stephen Greenblatt, 'Learning to curse: aspects of linguistic colonialism in the sixteenth century', in *Learning to Curse: essays in early modern culture* (London: Routledge, 1990), pp. 16–17.
2 *The Admirable Urquhart: Selected Writings*, ed. and introduced by Richard Boston (London: Gordon Fraser, 1975), p. 32.
3 ibid., p. 102.
4 ibid., pp. 115–6.
5 ibid., p. 116–21.
6 ibid., p. 125.
7 ibid., p. 137.
8 Ephraim Chambers, *Cyclopaedia*, I: xvi. Cited in Robert De Maria Jr, *Johnson's 'Dictionary' and the Language of Learning* (Oxford University Press, 1986), p. 5.
9 Cited in Tony Crowley, *The Politics of Discourse: the Standard Language Question in British Cultural Debates* (London: Macmillan, 1989), p. 83.

Chapter Six

1 Archbishop R.C. Trench, *On the Study of Words* (London, 1851).
2 Valentin Volesinov, *Marxism and the Philosophy of Language* (1930; London; Seminar Press 1973), p. 740.
3 E.P. Marsh, *Lectures on the English Language* (New York, 1860).

4 Joseph Priestley, *A Course of Lectures on the Theory of Language and Universal Grammar* (London, 1762), p. 129.
5 Matthew Arnold (H.M. Inspector of Schools), *General Report on the Elementary Schools for the Year 1852.*
6 Cited in David Cairns and Shaun Richards, *Writing Ireland: Colonialism, Nationalism and Culture* (Manchester: Manchester University Press 1988), p. 44.
7 Robert Lowe, *Primary and Classical Education* (London, 1867).
8 Henry Sweet, *The Sounds of English* (Oxford, 1908), p. 7.
9 Tony Crowley, *The Politics of Discourse*, p. 159.
10 Emily Brontë, *Wutnering Heights*, (1847; reprinted, Harmondsworth: Penguin 1965), p. 338.
11 *Political Register*, 6 December 1817, col. 1094.
12 Charles Dickens, *The Pickwick Papers* (1837; reprinted, Oxford: Oxford University Press 1948), p. 149.
13 ibid., p. 11.
14 Charlotte Brontë, *Jane Eyre* (1847; reprinted, Harmondsworth: Penguin, 1966), p. 141.
15 Thomas Hardy, *Far From the Madding Crowd* (1874; reprinted, Penguin: Harmondsworth 1978), p. 70–1.
16 Virginia Woolf, *A Room of One's Own* (1929; reprinted London: Grafton 1977, p. 78.
17 ibid., p. 83.
18 Susan Sellers (ed.), *Writing Differences: Readings from the Seminar of Hélène Cixous* (Milton Keynes: Open University Press, 1988), p. 3.
19 See S. McConnell-Ginet (ed.), *Women and Language in Literature and Society* (New York: Praeger, 1982).

Chapter Seven

1 The Bank of England, established in 1694, had already made a limited use of banknotes for discounting bills, making advances on commodities, and buying precious metals.
2 Quoted in Ellen Merksins Wood, *The Pristine Culture of Capitalism* (London: Verso, 1991), p. 82.
3 ibid., p. 84.
4 Constantine Caffentzis, *Clipped Coins, Abused Words and Civil Government: John Locke's Philosophy of Money* (New York: Autonomedia, 1989), p. 22.
5 Charles Dickens, *Our Mutual Friend* (1865; reprinted, Harmondsworth: Penguin, 1971), pp. 159–160.
6 ibid., p. 244.
7 ibid., p. 366.
8 John Ruskin, *Munera Pulveris: Six Essays on the Elements of Political Economy* (London, 1894), p. 76.
9 Marcel Mauss, *The Gift: Forms and Functions of Exchange in Archaic Societies*, tr. Ian Cunnison. (London: Cohen and West 1954), p. 31.

Chapter Eight

1 Charles Dickens, *Hard Times* (1854; reprinted, Harmondsworth: Penguin 1969), p. 50.
2 George Orwell, 'Politics and the English language', in *The Collected Essays, Journalism and Letters of George Orwell; Volume 4, 1945–50* (Harmondsworth: Penguin, 1978), p. 16.
3 'Appendix: the principles of Newspeak', in *The Penguin Complete Novels of George Orwell* (Harmondsworth Penguin 19), p. 917.
4 Orwell, 'Politics and the English language', p. 166.
5 Michael Herr, *Dispatches* (London: Picador, 1978), p. 48.
6 Tom Harrisson, *Living through the Blitz* (Harmondsworth: Penguin, 1978), p. 323.
7 Jean-François Lyotard, *The Postmodern Condition*, tr. Geoff Bennington (Manchester: Manchester University Press, 1984), p. 4.
8 Jean-François Lyotard, *Just Gaming*, tr. Wead Godzich (Manchester: Manchester University Press), p. 51.

BIBLIOGRAPHY

Abrams, M. H., *A Glossary of Literary Terms* (Harcourt Brace Jovanovich, Fort Worth 1993)

Aeschylus, *The Oresteian Trilogy*, tr. Philip Vellacott (Penguin, Harmondsworth 1956)

Anonymous, 'In adoration of Nature the Morning pawn 10th & 11th October 1976', Rod Mengham and John Wilkinson (eds.), *Equofinality*, no. 2 (1984)

Aristotle, *De Interpretatione*, tr. H. P. Cook (Loeb, London 1938)

Arnold, Matthew (H.M. Inspector of Schools), *General Report on the Elementary Schools for the year 1852*

Baigent, Michael and Leigh, Richard, *The Dead Sea Scrolls Deception* (Jonathan Cape, London 1991)

Bakhtin, Mikhail, *The Dialogic Imagination*, tr. C. Emerson and M. Holquist (University of Texas, Austin 1981)

Bassnett, Susan, *Translation Studies* (Routledge, London 1991)

Benjamin, Walter, *Illuminations*, tr. Harry Zohn (Jonathan Cape, London 1970)

Bernal, Martin, *Cadmean Letters: The Transmission of the Alphabet to the Aegean and Further West before 1400 B.C.* (Eisenbrauns, Winona Lake 1990)

Bleuler, Eugen, *Dementia Praecox or the Group of Schizophrenias* (International Universities Press, New York 1950)

Bonfante, L., *Etruscan* (British Museum, London 1990)

Brecht, Bertolt, *The Messingkauf Dialogues*, tr. John Willett (Methuen, London 1956)

Brontë, Charlotte, *Jane Eyre* (Penguin, Harmondsworth 1966)

Brontë, Emily, *Wuthering Heights* (Penguin, Harmondsworth 1965)

Burroughs, William S., *The Adding Machine: Collected Essays* (John Calder, London 1985)

Caffentzis, Constantine, *Clipped Coins, Abused Words and Civil Government: John Locke's Philosophy of Money* (Autonomedia, New York 1989)

Cairns, David and Richards, Shaun, *Writing Ireland: Colonialism, Nationalism and Culture* (Manchester University Press, Manchester 1988)

Chambers, Ephraim, *Cyclopaedia: or, an Universal Dictionary of Arts and Sciences* (London 1728)

Cobbett, William, *A Grammar of the English Language*, C. C. Nickerson and U. W. Osborne (eds.), (Amsterdam 1983)

Cook, B. F., *Greek Inscriptions* (British Museum, London 1987)

Crowley, Tony, *The Politics of Discourse: The Standard Language Question in British Cultural Debates* (Macmillan, London 1989)

Damasio, Antonio R. and Hanna, 'Brain and Language', *Scientific American*, vol. 267, no. 3 (September, 1992)

Debord, Guy, *The Society of the Spectacle* (Black and Red, Detroit 1983)

De Maria Jr, Robert, *Johnson's 'Dictionary' and the Language of Learning* (Oxford University Press, Oxford 1986)

Derrida, Jacques, *Positions*, tr. Alan Bass (Chicago University Press, Chicago 1981)
Dickens, Charles, *Hard Times* (Penguin, Harmondsworth 1969) *Our Mutual Friend* (Penguin, Harmondsworth 1971) *The Pickwick Papers* (Oxford University Press, Oxford 1948)
Eisenman, R. H., *Maccabees, Zadokites, Christians and Qumran* (E. J. Brill, Leiden 1983)
Gaur, Albertine, *A History of Writing* (British Library Reference Division Publications, London 1984)
Gelb, I. J., *A Study of Writing* (Chicago University Press, Chicago 1963)
Goldhill, Simon, *Reading Greek Tragedy* (Cambridge University Press, Cambridge 1986)
Golding, William, *The Inheritors* (Faber & Faber, London 1955)
Goody, Jack, *The Interface Between the Written and the Oral* (Cambridge University Press, Cambridge 1987)
Greenblatt, Stephen, *Learning to Curse: Essays in Early Modern Culture* (Routledge, London 1990) *Renaissance Self-Fashioning* (University of Chicago Press, Chicago 1980)
Hardy, Thomas, *Far From the Madding Crowd* (Penguin, Harmondsworth 1978)
Harris, James, *Hermes or a Philosophical Inquiry Concerning Universal Grammar* (H. Woodfall, London 1986)
Harris, Roy, *The Origin of Writing* (Duckworth, London 1986)
Harrisson, Tom, *Living through the Blitz* (Penguin, Harmondsworth 1978)
Healey, John F., *The Early Alphabet* (British Museum, London 1990)
Herodutus, *The Histories*, tr. Aubrey de Selincourt (Penguin, Harmondsworth 1954)
Herr, Michael, *Dispatches* (Picador, London 1978)
Hoban, Russell, *Riddley Walker* (Jonathan Cape, London 1980)
Holquist, Michael, *Bakhtin and His World* (Routledge, London 1990)
Homer, *The Iliad*, tr. Robert Fagles (Penguin, Harmondsworth 1990)
Horapollo, Nilous, *Hieroglyphics*, tr. A. T. Cory (London 1840)
Jameson, Fredric, *Postmodernism, or the Cultural Logic of Late Capitalism* (Verso, London 1991)
Jefferey, L. H., *The Local Scripts of Archaic Greece* (Oxford University Press, Oxford 1961)
Johnson, Samuel, *Dictionary of the English Language* (W. Strachan, London 1755)
Joyce, James, 'The Dead', from *Dubliners* (Penguin, Harmondsworth 1956)
Khalifa, Mohammed, *The Sublime Qur'an and Orientalism* (Longman, London 1983)
Knowlson, James, *Universal Language Schemes in England and France 1600–1800* (University of Toronto Press, Toronto 1975)
Lawless, Hon. Emily, *The Story of Ireland* (T. Fisher Unwin, London 1888)
Lowe-Evans, Mary, *Crimes Against Fecundity: Joyce and Population Control* (Syracuse University Press, London 1989)
Lyotard, Jean-Francois and Jean-Loup Thebaud, *Just Gaming*, tr. Wlad Godzich (Manchester University Press, Manchester 1985)
Lyotard, Jean-Francois, *The Postmodern Condition: A Report on Knowledge*, tr. Geoff Bennington and Brian Massumi (Manchester University Press, Manchester 1984)
Mallory, J. P., *In Search of the Indo-Europeans: Language Archaeology and Myth* (Thames and Hudson, London 1989)
Marsh, G. P., *Lectures on the English Language* (New York 1860)
Mauss, Marcel, *The Gift: Forms and Functions of Exchange in Archaic Societies*, tr. Ian Cunnison (Cohen and West, London 1954)
McConnell-Ginet, S. (ed.), *Women and Language in Literature and Society* (Praeger, New York 1980)
Meiksins Wood, Ellen, *The Pristine Culture of Capitalism* (Verso, London 1991)
Moretti, Franco, *Signs Taken for Wonders: Essays in the Sociology of Literary Forms* (Verso, London 1983)
Ong, Walter J., *Orality and Literacy* (Methuen, London 1982)
O'Rourke, Rev. John, *History of the Great Irish Famine of 1847* (Dublin 1875)
Orwell, George, 'Politics and the English Language' in *The Collected Essays, Journalism and Letters of George Orwell, vol. 4., 1945–50* (Penguin, Harmondsworth 1978)
1984 in *The Complete Novels of George Orwell* (Penguin, Harmondsworth 1983)
Parsons, James, *The Remains of Japhet, being historical enquiries into the affinity and origins of the European Languages* (London 1767)

Pedersen, H., *The Discovery of Language: Linguistic Science in the Nineteenth Century*, tr. J. W. Spargo (Bloomington 1959)

Plato, 'Gorgias' in *The Dialogues of Plato*, tr. Benjamin Jowett (Oxford University Press, Oxford 1892)

Phaedrus and Letters VII and VIII, tr. Walter Hamilton (Penguin, Harmondsworth 1975)

Powell, Barry B., *Homer and the Origin of the Greek Alphabet* (Cambridge University Press, Cambridge 1991)

Priestley, Joseph, *A Course of Lectures on the Theory of Language and Universal Grammar* (London 1762)

Renfrew, Colin, *Archaeology and Language: the Puzzle of Indo-European Origins* (Jonathan Cape, London 1987)

Richards, Thomas, *The Commodity Culture of Victorian England* (Verso, London 1991)

Rodefer, Stephen, *Four Lectures* (The Figures, Berkeley, Ca. 1982)

Ronell, Avital, *The Telephone Book: Technology, Schizophrenia, Electric Speech* (University of Nebraska Press, Lincoln Nebraska 1989)

Ruskin, John, *Munera Pulveris: Six Essays on the Elements of Political Economy* (London 1894)

Sapir, Edward, *Language: An Introduction to the Study of Speech* (Rupert Hart Davis, London 1921)

Sasanuma, S., 'Acquired dyslexia in Japanese: clinical features and underlying mechanisms', in M. Coltheart, K. Paterson and J. C. Marshall (eds.), *Deep Dyslexia* (Routledge and Kegan Paul, London 1980)

Sass, B., *The Genesis of the Alphabet and its Development in the Second Millenium B.C.* (Otto Harrassowitz, Wiesbaden 1988)

Saussure, Ferdinand de, *Course in General Linguistics*, tr. Roy Harris (Duckworth, London 1983)

Schmandt-Besserat, D., 'The Earliest Precursor of Writing', *Scientific American*, vol. 238, no. 6 (June 1978)

Segal, Charles, *Interpreting Greek Tragedy: Myth, Poetry Text* (Cornell University Press, Ithaca 1986)

Sellers, Susan, (ed.), *Writing Differences: Readings from the Seminar of Hélenè Cixous* (Open University Press, Milton Keynes 1988)

Shakespeare, William, *Coriolanus*, ed. Philip Brockbank (Methuen, London 1976)

Hamlet, ed. Harold Jenkins (Methuen, London 1982)

King Lear, ed. Kenneth Muir (Methuen, London 1972)

Macbeth, ed. Kenneth Muir (Methuen, London 1951)

Shell, Marc, *The Economy of Literature* (John Hopkins University Press, Baltimore 1978)

Money, Language and Thought (University of California Press, Berkeley 1982)

Smith, Nigel (ed.), *A Collection of Ranter Writings from the Seventeenth Century* (Junction Books, London 1983)

Sophocles, *The Theban Plays*, tr. E. F. Watling (Penguin, Harmondsworth 1947)

Starr, Chester, *The Birth of Athenian Democracy: the Assembly in the Fifth Century B.C.* (Oxford University Press, New York 1991)

Stephens, John and Waterhouse, Ruth, *Literature, Language and Change* (Routledge, London 1990)

Sweet, Henry, *The Sounds of English* (Clarendon Press, Oxford 1908)

Trench, Archbishop R.C., *On the Study of Words* (London 1851)

Urquhart, Sir Thomas, *The Admirable Urquhart: Selected Writings*, ed. Richard Boston (Gordon Fraser, London 1975)

Vernant, Jean-Pierre, and Vidal-Naquet, Pierre, *Myth and Tragedy in Ancient Greece* (Harvester, Brighton 1981)

Volosinov, Valentin, *Marxism and the Philosophy of Langauge* (Seminar Press, London 1973)

Wallace, Marjorie, *The Silent Twins* (Penguin, Harmondsworth 1987)

Winkler, John J. (ed.), *Nothing to Do with Dionysus: Athenian Drama* (Princeton University Press, Princeton 1990)

Woolf, Virginia, *A Room of One's Own* (Grafton, London 1977)

INDEX

'abecedary', 41
Académie Française, 148
advertisements, 161–2, 164
Aeschylus, *Oresteia*, 81, 83–6
Akkadians, 110
Albanian, 62
Alexandria, Library of, 102
Al Mina, 46
alphabets, 29, 30, 40–50, 64, 77, 103; Arabic, 40; Aramaic, 40–3 *passim*; Greek, 41–50 *passim*, 61; Euboean, 46–7; Ionic, 44, 47; Hebrew, 41–3 *passim*; Phoenician, 41–7 *passim*; Roman, 40; runic, 40; universal, 103
Anatolian group of languages, 58
aoidoi, 49
Arabian Nights, 120
Arabic, 61, 69–70, 166
Aramaic, 42, 72
Aristotle, 29, 30
Armenian, 46, 58–9
Arnold, Matthew, 125–6, 138
Assyrian, 40
Ataturk, Kemal, 34
Athens, 47, 78–80, 83–9 *passim*
Avestan/*Avesta*, 60

Bacon, Francis, 103, 148
Balkans, 62
Balts/Baltic, 54, 63
Beck, Cave, *The Universal Character*, 103
bi-graphism, 40
bilingualism, 56, 166
bills, 150
Bleuler, Eugen, 21–2
Boghazköy, 58
boustrophedon, 45
brain, 17–26; language centres, 17–19 *passim*; mediation system, 19; PET scans, 19, 21; perisylvian sectors, anterior, 18, 19, posterior, 17, 19
Brecht, Bertolt, 95
British Isles, 125
Brontë, Anne, 136
Brontë, Charlotte, *Jane Eyre*, 136
Brontë, Emily, 136; *Wuthering Heights*, 130
Bronze Age, 47
burial practices, 68–9
Byblos, 44

Cadmean Letters, 43–4, 48
Caffentzis, Constantine, 149–50
Cawdrey, Robert, *Table Alphabeticall*, 111
Celts/Celtic, 54, 55, 64, 67, 125, 138, 168
centum/satem pattern, 55
Chambers, Ephraim, *Cyclopaedia*, 112, 113
Champollion, Jean-François, 39
Chartists, 120, 123
Cherokee, 33
China/Chinese, 33, 40, 148
Christianity, 61, 70, 72–3, 86, 113–14
Cixous, Hélène, 138
class, social, 7, 127–8, 130, 132–4, 148–9, 178
Cobbett, William, *Grammar*, 130–2; *Le Tuteur anglais*, 131–2
Cockeram, Henry, *English Dictionarie*, 111
coinage, 143–4, 146, 149–50
Columbus, Christopher, 101
computers, 174, 176, 177
Conrad, Joseph, 156–7; *Heart of Darkness*, 156; *Nostromo*, 156
Coppe, Abiezer, 101
Cornwall/Cornish, 64, 168
Crete, 45, 62

Cubelli, Roberto, 26
Dalgarno, George, 103
Davis, Thomas, 126–7
Dead Sea Scrolls, 42, 70, 72–3
Deioces, King of the Medes, 144
democracy, 47, 77–80, 83
Derrida, Jacques, 32
dialect, 128
Dickens, Charles, 147–8, 152–4; *American Notes*, 148; *Hard Times*, 162, 165; *Our Mutual Friend*, 150–4 *passim*; *Pickwick Papers*, 132–5
dictionaries, 110–16
'Dipylon oinochoe', 48
Disraeli, Benjamin, *Sybil*, 127
Donnelly, Ignatius, *The American People's Money*, 155
dyslexia, 34

education, 102, 119–20, 127–8
Egypt, 30–1, 35, 37, 39, 40, 57–8, 112
encyclopaedias, 111
English, 7, 34, 54, 56, 103, 111–20, 125, 157–8, 162, 164, 165
Esperanto, 169–70
Essenes, 72
Etruscans, 47–8, 64
Euboea, 46–7
Euripides, 77, 84, 136
Europe, 40, 165; Eastern, 158

family tree model, 4, 7, 54, 105, 109
Finnish, 166
Finno-Ugric, 57
French, 54, 116–18, 148, 164; Revolution, 117, 123, 124, 154
Freud, Sigmund, 22–3

Gaelic, 125, 126
Galfridus Grammaticus, *Promptorium parvulorum sive clericorum*, 110–11
'games, language', 174–6 *passim*
Gathas, 60–1
Gelb, I.J., 46
gender issues, 7, 83–5, 135–9, 178
Germanic/Germans, 40, 54, 57, 63, 64, 66, 67
Gibbons, June & Jennifer, 24–5; *Pepsi-Cola Addict*, 25
Gimbutas, Marija, 68
glyphs, 32–3, 37
Goethe, Johann Wolfgang von, 126
gold, 146, 147, 155
Goldhill, Simon, 91
Golding, William, *Inheritors*, 4–5, 7, 12
Gothic, 46, 54, 64
grammar, 102, 119–20, 130–2, 137; universal, 102–10
Greek, 35, 39, 41–50 *passim*, 57, 61–2, 66, 67, 77–89 *passim*, 119, 167; proto-, 61–2
Grimm brothers, 126
Gutenberg, Johannes, 37, 144
Gyges, King of Lydia, 143

Habbakuk Commentary, 72
Hamitic, 57
Hardy, Thomas, *Far From the Madding Crowd*, 136–7
Harrisson, Tom, *Living Through the Blitz*, 172–3
Hartlib, Samuel, 103
Hauser, Kaspar, 57
Hebrew, 41–3 *passim*, 72
Hegel, Georg Wilhelm Friedrich, 126, 176
Herder, Gottfried, 126
Herodotus, 39, 43–4, 48–9, 57, 62, 63, 67, 144
Herr, Michael, *Dispatches*, 171
Hesiod, 85
hieroglyphs, 37, 39, 40, 112
history, 8, 12, 117
Hittite, 55, 58–60 *passim*, 66
Hoban, Russell, *Riddley Walker*, 6–7, 12
Homer, 36, 47–9 *passim*, 61, 62
Horapollo, *Hieroglyphica*, 37, 39
Hurrians, 60
hydronymy, 62

ideology, 57, 62, 65, 68, 69, 72, 83, 85, 92, 170, 173, 175, 178
Illyrian, 62
Indic, 59, 60, 66
Indo-European, 53–69, 125; proto-, 53, 55, 65–6, 69, 164–5
Ionians/Ionic, 44, 47
Iranian, 35, 60–2 *passim*, 66, 67
Ireland/Irishness, 8–9, 11–12, 64, 126–7, 138; Famine, 11–12
Islam, 69–70, 86
Israel, 42–3
Italic, 55, 64

Japanese, 33, 34, 40
Japhetic, 57
Jews, 70, 86
Johnson, Samuel, *Dictionary*, 111, 113–16, 119, 131, 143, 153–4
Jones, Sir William, 54
Joyce, James, *The Dead*, 8–9, 11, 12; *Finnegans Wake*, 147, 161; *Ulysses*, 156

Kersey, John, *New English Dictionary*, 111
Khlobystina, Maryana, 68–9
Kikkuli the Mittani, 60
Kildare Place Society, 127
Koran, 69–70
Kristeva, Julia, 137–9 *passim*
Kurgan culture, 68

Lacan, Jacques, 17, 21
Latin, 45, 70, 102, 103, 119–20, 165, 167
Law, John, 148
Leavis, F.R., 156
Leeds Grammar School, 119
literacy, 26, 36
literature, 47–9, 61, 154–6, 178 *see also individual headings*; tragedy
Lithuanian, 63
Locke, John, 149–52 *passim*
Lodwick, Francis, *A Common Writing*, 103
Lowe, Robert, *Primary & Classical Education*, 127–8
Lowndes, William, 149, 150
Luwian, 59
Lyotard, Jean-François, *The Postmodern Condition*, 174–7 *passim*

Malaya, 40
Marsh, G.P., *Lectures*, 124–5
Marshall, John, 26
Marx, Karl, 147
Mass-Observation, 172–3
Mauss, Marcel, 158
Melanesia, 158
Mesavouno, Thera, 48
Mesopotamia, 34
Mitanni, 59–60, 66
money, 143, 146–51, 155, 158 *see also* coinage; paper, 147–8
Myceneans, 62
myths, 30, 35–6, 57–8, 61, 66–8 *passim*

narrative, 11, 175–6
National Society, 127
nationalism, 7, 42, 102, 125–7, 157, 178
Neanderthals, 5, 7
de Nebrija, Antonio, *Gramatica*, 101, 102
Neolithic period, 68–9
Nestor, cup of, 47–8
Newton, Sir Isaac, 149
Norse, 66
numeracy, 35

Ong, Walter J., 37, 123
oracles, 86–7
O'Rourke, Rev. John, 11
Orwell, George, 168–70; *1984*, 169; 'Politics and the English Language', 170
ostracism, 89–90

Palaic, 59
Palestine, 61
Papua, 158
papyrus, 39, 44
Phoenician, 41–5 *passim*
Philips, Edward, *A New Worlde of English Words*, 111
philology, 123–4, 132, 134
Phrygian, 55, 58
physiology, 13, 17–21
pictograms, 32–3
Pithekoussai, 48
Plato, 29, 50; *Phaedrus*, 30–1
poésie blanche, 156
Polish, 157, 166–7
'political correctness', 139
politics, 7, 11, 77–80, 83, 126–7, 168–9
Polo, Marco, 148
Priestley, Joseph, 125
pronunciation, 34
'proto-lexikon', 65–6, 69
Prussian, Old, 63
Psammetichus, King, 57–8
psychoanalysis, 21–2, 87

Rabelais, 108
race, 7, 139, 178
referential function, 147
religion, 7, 56–7, 59, 60, 65, 66, 68–73 *passim*, 86–7, 113, 124
Renfrew, Colin, 56–7, 64
rhapsodoi, 49
rhyme, 24
Rodefer, Stephen, 53
Romans, 47, 64, 66, 67, 165
Rosetta Stone, 39
rote-learning, 119, 127, 128
Rousseau, Jean Jacques, 29
Royal Society, 103, 148–9, 153, 162
Ruskin, John, *Munera Pulveris*, 154–6 *passim*

Samaritans, 42
Sanskrit, 54, 59, 63
Sapir, Edward, 4
Sarmatians, 62
Saussure, Ferdinand de, 29, 30, 147
Saxons, 164
Scaliger, Joseph, 57
schizophrenia, 21–4
Schleicher, August, 54

Schmidt, Johannes, 55
Scotland/Scotch, 64, 125 *see also* Gaelic
scripts, 30, 32–4, 37, 39–50; Arabic, 34, 41; Aramaic, 40–3 *passim*; cuneiform, 40, 41; demotic, 39; Greek, 41; Hebrew, 41–3 *passim*; hieratic, 39; Latin, 34, 45; Linear A, 62; Linear B, 61–2; Proto-Canaanite/Sinaitic, 41–2; Ugaritic, 41–2
Scythians, 62, 67–8
Semitic, 42, 57
Sequoyah (John Guess), 33
Shakespeare, William, 87, 91–7; *Coriolanus*, 97; *Hamlet*, 29, 96; *King Lear*, 96–7; *Macbeth*, 92–5; *Richard III*, 114–15
Sinai, 41
Slavic, 54, 57, 62–3
Socrates, 30–1, 49, 50, 78, 79
Sophists, 78–9
Sophocles, *Oedipus Tyrannos*, 87–91
speech, 17, 25, 26, 29–31, 34, 128
Sprat, Thomas, 103, 148
syllabary, 33, 40–1, 61
Syria, 41

taboos, 35
Tacitus, 64, 66
Tanzania, 40
technology, 173–4, 176, 178; information, 31, 174, 177
telephone, 173–4
Thackeray, William Makepeace, *Vanity Fair*, 116–20
Thamus, King, 30–1
Thebes, 48, 88–91
Theuth, 30–1, 37
Thracian, 62
Thrax, Dionysius, *Art of Letters*, 102
Tocharian, 55–6
trade, 35, 56, 143, 150
tragedy, 80–97, 101
translatability, 174, 176
translation, 126–7, 133, 158, 162, 164–70 *passim*, 173, 178
Trench, Archbishop, R.C., 124
Turkish, 34
twins, 24–5
tyranny, 143–4

United States, 123, 131, 139, 155
universal language, 103–10, 157–8, 168–70
untranslatability, 126–7
Urquhart, Sir Thomas, 103, 105–10; *Logopandecteison*, 105; *Pantochronochanon*, 105–6

Varro, *De Lingua Latina*, 102
Vedas, 59
Vernant, Jean-Pierre, 80–1
Volosinov, Valentin, *Marxism & the Philosophy of Language*, 124
vowels, 26, 43, 44

Wales/Welsh, 64, 125–6, 168
Wallace, Marjorie, 25
war, 170, 171; English Civil, 105; Gulf, 171; Second World, 172–3; Vietnam, 170–1; Yugoslav civil, 171
Watts, Isaac, 131
wave theory, 55
Wells, David A., *The Silver Question*, 146; *Robinson Crusoe's Money*, 146
Whorf, Benjamin Lee, 12
Wilkins, John, 103
Wittgenstein, Ludwig, 174–5
women, 69, 83–5 *passim*, 135–9
Woolf, Virginia, *Room of One's Own*, 137
writing, 17, 25, 26, 29–50, 69–70, 77, 102, 112, 143, 144, 173, 178; logographic, 34, 39–41; phonographic, 33–5 *passim*, 40, 41; *see also* scripts
Wulfilas, Bishop, 64

Young, Thomas, 53

Zamenhof, Ludwig, 169
Zarathustra, 60, 61
Zoroastrianism, 60–1

Fontana Modern Masters

Piaget

Second Edition

Margaret A. Boden

'A marvellous starting-point, easily the best available, for anyone setting out to understand Piaget.'

Peter Bryant, *London Review of Books*

Jean Piaget (1896–1980) is world-famous for his work in child psychology. His detailed studies of the development of thinking from infancy to adolescence, on which he based his theory of intelligence as interiorized action and his vision of the mind as a system of self-regulating structures responsive to the subject's interaction with the environment, have not only influenced academic psychologists but have led to radical changes in school curricula and classroom organization. Yet Piaget regarded himself as a biologist and philosopher (a 'genetic epistemologist') first and a developmental psychologist only second.

In this clear critical acount of Piaget's work, Margaret Boden discusses the biological and philosophical issues that influenced Piaget's psychology. She relates his theoretical identification of equilibration with cybernetic control to current work on artificial intelligence. And in this revised edition, she discusses recent evidence for epigenesis, new connectionist models of psychological development, dynamic systems theory and A-Life, and assesses the resilience of Piaget's standing as an intellectual force in psychology. While he may well have underestimated the abilities of infants, his depiction of mental development as ordered structural change still reigns unchallenged in the field, and his ideas remain the obligatory grounding for any student seeking to come to terms with the complex field of child psychology.

ISBN 0 00 686331 0

Fontana Modern Masters
Editor: Frank Kermode

Chomsky

Third Edition

John Lyons

Chomsky's contribution to the study of language has, over the last four decades, been enormous, and has influenced those working in many disciplines, including the other cognitive sciences. Language is, arguably, an even more distinctively human characteristic than intelligence, and the thousands of different human languages are, according to Chomsky, cut to the same general pattern. This pattern is determined, he claims, by innate structuring principles which only human beings possess. Chomsky's search for the universal in language has revitalized the question of the relationship between language and mind, and has provided a powerful new tool, generative grammar, for students of language.

In this Third Edition of his concise, accessible introduction to Chomsky's work, John Lyons has added an extensive final chapter which seeks to assess the continuing ramifications of the Chomskyan Revolution in linguistics today. He has also thoroughly updated the bibliographies – both of Chomsky's own prolific output and of the multiplying secondary material – and the biographical note, in order fully to arm any prospective explorer of Chomsky's *oeuvre* with all the relevant resources they may need.

'John Lyons' book on Chomsky is simply the best short introduction in the English language. It is within the grasp of an intelligent layman. Anyone who reads it will understand the elements of transformational grammar, and be able to follow current controversies.'

Leonard Jackson, *Times Educational Supplement*

'Lyons' account is itself a minor modern masterpiece of compression and clarity.'

Alan Ryan, *New Society*

ISBN 0 00 686229 2

Fontana Press

Fontana Movements and Ideas
Series Editor: Justin Wintle

The Psychoanalytic Movement

The Cunning of Unreason

Second edition

Ernest Gellner

'Certainly the most powerful attempt so far to situate Freud in the wide history of European ideas.' PERRY ANDERSON, *New Left Review*

In this bracing and ebullient study, Ernest Gellner explains why Freud's ideas spread so far and why, whether we like it or not, we are all Freudians now, bathing in the balm of his 'whole climate of opinion'.

'In a stylish, witty and deceptively readable book, Gellner exposes the secular religious nature of the psychoanalytic enterprise. He admits that a compelling, charismatic belief must possess more than merely the promise of succour in a plague and links with the background convictions of the age.' ANTHONY CLARE, *Nature*

'The puzzling survival of the Victorian relic, psychoanalysis, is what this brilliant, caustic and infuriating little essay sets out to explain in a biting critique of the movement's pretensions.' MICHAEL IGNATIEFF

'One of those iconoclastic masterpieces of sceptical good sense and fine intelligence that you might come across once in ten years if you're lucky.' *New Statesman*

'This is the first determined effort to account for a very odd historical and sociological phenomenon in realistic and meaningful terms... and it makes very good sense. Gellner is incisive, agreeable to read and often witty.' HANS EYSENCK, *Institute of Psychiatry Journal*

'In this brilliant book... Gellner describes powerfully, and in the most brightly coloured prose, the causality of Freudian dogma. In doing so he destroys its scientific claims, and devalues its morality.'
ROGER SCRUTON, *The Times*

'A piece of sustainedly brilliant and witty writing.' *Sunday Times*

0 00 686300 0

Modern Essays

Frank Kermode

Frank Kermode is widely regarded as the most distinguished literary critic in the English language. In this collection of some of his best short pieces he considers poets and dancers, obscenity and modernity, and such diverse figures as J. D. Salinger and Muriel Spark, D. H. Lawrence and Samuel Beckett. Kermode consistently demonstrates that criticism of a high order can indeed 'defy the action of time'.

'In almost any review, Professor Kermode comes up with some shining new key to turn in the subject's lock' (*Listener*). He is 'one of the two or three outstanding English critics of his generation' (*Observer*). His reviews 'are definitely among those responsible for sending people into the bookshops and libraries' (*Times Literary Supplement*). In fact, 'there is no better critic writing in English than Kermode at his best' (*New Republic*).

Frank Kermode has been Northcliffe Professor of Modern English Literature at University College London, King Edward VII Professor of English Literature at Cambridge, and Charles Eliot Norton Professor of Poetry at Harvard. He is the General Editor of the Modern Masters and Masterguides series, and of the Oxford Authors. He is a Foreign Honorary Member of the American Academy of Arts and Sciences, an Officer de l'Ordre des Arts et des Sciences, and has received several honorary degrees. He now lives in Cambridge.

ISBN 0 00 686206 3

Fontana Press

Fontana Modern Masters
Series Editor: Frank Kermode

Heidegger

Second Edition

George Steiner

No philosopher has aroused such passion, such diametrically opposed views about his status in the history of thought as Martin Heidegger (1889–1976); what you think about him tends to reveal what you think about being in the twentieth century. His champions see his work as elemental in this century's intellectual composition, and point to the imapct of this thought on a diversity of disciplines and movements, among them Sartrean existentialism, linguistics, the 'structuralist' and 'hermeneutic' schools of textual interpretation, theology, Hellenic studies, poetics, and, indeed, literature itself. In the opposing camp, his detractors rule discussion of this thought futile: his writings being impenetrable, his questions sham, his insights banal, his doctrines false, his influence diastrous.

'It would be hard to imagine a better introduction to the work of philosopher Martin Heidegger than this book.' *New Republic*

'Whether readers or thinkers respond to Heidegger or not, some acquaintance with his thought is indispensable, and Dr Steiner has provided it beautifully.' *New Yorker*

'Steiner's short book, in its generosity of feeling and range of reference, is a continuous pleasure to read.'
New York Review of Books

ISBN 0 00 686247 0

Fontana Press